A Season of

Nature Poems for

Catholic Children

Summer

A Summer Season of Nature Poems for Catholic Children

Janet P. McKenzie, OCDS

A Race for Heaven Book

Biblio Resource Publications, Inc.
108½ S. Moore St.
Bessemer, MI 49911
2020

OTHER BOOKS IN THE
NATURE POEMS FOR
CATHOLIC CHILDREN SERIES:

*An Autumn Season of Nature Poems
for Catholic Children*

*A Winter Season of Nature Poems
for Catholic Children*

*A Spring Season of Nature Poems
for Catholic Children*

OTHER BOOKS BY JANET P. MCKENZIE
WWW.RACEFORHEAVEN.COM

STUDY GUIDES AND AIDS

✝ A Series of 20 Saint Study Guides for the saint books written by Mary Fabyan Windeatt (available as individual study guides or grade-level guides)

✝ *Graced Encounters with Mary Fabyan Windeatt's Saints: 344 Ways to Imitate the Holy Habits of Saints*

✝ *The Windeatt Dictionary: Pre-Vatican II Terms and Catholic Words from Mary Fabyan Windeatt's Saint Biographies*

✝ *Reading the Saints: Lists of Catholic Books for Children plus Book Collecting Tips for the Home and School Library, Second Edition*

✝ *Alternative Books Reports for Catholic Students*

✝ *The King of the Golden City Study Edition* (includes text and guide or individual guide available)

✝ *Outlaws of Ravenhurst Study Edition* (includes text and guide or individual guide available)

✝ *The Family that Overtook Christ Study Edition: Lessons in Sanctity from the Family of St. Bernard of Clairvaux* (includes text and guide)

✝ *By Cross and Anchor Study Edition: The Story of Frederic Baraga on Lake Superior* (includes text and guide)

RECONCILIATION/FIRST HOLY COMMUNION

✝ *A Reconciliation Reader-Retreat: Read-aloud Lessons, Stories, and Poems for Young Catholics Preparing for Confession*

✠ *Communion with the Saints, A Family Preparation Program for First Communion and Beyond in the Spirit of St. Therese*

✠ *The King of the Golden City Study Edition* (includes text and guide or individual guide available)

✠ *My First Communion Journal in Imitation of St. Therese, the Little Flower*

✠ *My First Communion Journal in Imitation of St. Paul: Putting on the Armor of God*

✠ *The Good Shepherd and His Little Lambs Study Edition: A First Communion Story-Primer*

SACRAMENT OF CONFIRMATION

✠ *A Confirmation Reader-Retreat: Read-Aloud Lessons, Stories, and Poems for Young Catholics*

✠ *The Family that Overtook Christ Study Edition: Lessons in Sanctity from the Family of St. Bernard of Clairvaux* (adult and teens)

ST. JOSEPH

✠ *The Month of St. Joseph: Prayers and Practices for Each Day of March in Imitation of the Virtues of St. Joseph* (adult)

✠ *Devotion to St. Joseph: Read-Aloud Stories, Poems, and Prayers for Catholic Children*

OTHER BOOKS

✠ *I Talk with God: The Art of Prayer and Meditation for Catholic Children*

✠ *Bedtime Bible Stories for Catholic Children: Loving Jesus through His Word*

This book is dedicated to my grandchildren: Ali, Grace, Norah, Ethan, Katie, Jon, Jacob, Elena, and all those to come.

Nature is so much more fun and inspiring when I explore it with you.

With great love,
Nana

ACKNOWLEDGEMENTS

Dust Jacket Design by Joshua Kodis

Dust Jacket Photo ©vvvita iStockPhoto.com

Dust Jacket Graphics ©Aleksander Guvrilovic
iStockPhoto.com

Divider Page Illustration ©Myatta iStockPhoto.com

June 7 Illustration ©Denise Fortado
Shutterstock.com

June 25 Illustration ©Morphart Creation
ShutterStock.com

July 5 Illustration ©Lukutina Olesya
Shutterstock.com

July 7 Illustration © R. Wilairat ShutterStock.com

July 20 Illustration ©Bodor Tivadar
ShutterStock.com

August 4 Illustration ©Melok ShutterStock.com

August 12 Illustration ©BigMouse ShutterStock.com

August 19 Illustration ©Barashkova Natalia
ShutterStock.com

"To the Immaculate Heart of Mary"
© 2019 Janet P. McKenzie

But now ask the beasts to teach you,
the birds of the air to tell you;
Or speak to the earth to instruct you,
and the fish of the sea to inform you.
Which of all these does not know
that the hand of God has done this?

Job 12:7-9

And Nature, the old nurse, took
The child upon her knee,
Saying: "Here is a story-book
thy Father has written for thee."

"Come, wander with me," she said,
"Into regions yet untrod;
And read what is still unread
In the manuscripts of God."

And he wandered away and away
With Nature, the dear old nurse,
Who sang to him night and day
The rhymes of the universe.

From "The Fiftieth Birthday of Agassiz" by
Henry Wadsworth Longfellow (1807-1882)

TABLE OF CONTENTS

PREFACE

Throughout my childhood, my father worked as a manager in the Michigan State Parks system. We moved every three or four years to a different park within Michigan's Upper Peninsula. Even as a young child, I remember spending long days and evenings outdoors—in the woods, on the beach, in the yard. Many of these memories include my siblings and neighborhood friends. But many are the times I spent alone at various "secret" places I had found, places I often escaped to in order to think deep-child thoughts—to communicate with God.

Although I hesitate to compare my experiences with those of a saint, St. Thérèse the Little Flower, describes similar experiences in *The Story of a Soul*: "I preferred to go *alone* and sit down on the grass bedecked with flowers, and then my thoughts became very profound indeed! Without knowing what it was to meditate, my soul was absorbed in real prayer" (SOS 37). St. Thérèse talks often of how she was inspired to love, praise, and understand the God that the book of nature opened to her.

As a Discalced Carmelite Secular, my life is focused on union with God. Like St. Augustine (yes, another saint comparison!), I searched for many years for God, in various places and circumstances. However, in my Carmelite journey of faith, I have discovered that God can be found within. He resides in our very souls—nearer to us than we are to ourselves. Yet, in my adult searching, I have found —just as in my childhood—that I often commune best with Him in natural environments. I feel His presence in the beauty and holy silence of nature. Surrounded by creation, my mind frees, my soul fills with gratitude, and my heart connects with our loving Creator.

Here too we are in good company with the saints. Both St. Teresa of Jesus and St. John of the Cross, Carmelite Doctors, often used the natural world as a conduit to God:

✝ "It helped me also to look at fields, or water, or flowers. In these things I found a remembrance of the creator. I mean that they awakened and recollected me and served as a book and reminded me of my ingratitude and sins" (St. Teresa of Jesus, *Life* 9.5).

✝ "Beholding in creation a trace of the divine beauty, power, and loving wisdom, John could not easily resist the enchantment of nature. . . . He would take the friars out to the mountains . . . so that each might pass the day alone there 'in solitary prayer'" (*The Collected Works of St. John of the Cross* 26).

Many are the quotations we could cite from saints, popes, theologians, the Catechism, and Scripture that support an appreciation of the natural world as an important dimension of our relationship with God. However, we also need an awareness of the errors of the "New Age" movement, the theological problems with "nature worship", the heresy of pantheism, and an understanding that God does not depend upon creation for His identity to direct our path. If you are concerned or curious about these issues, please review the Appendix of this book.

In this series, we embark upon a study of nature and God in nature by reading aloud one poem per day, spending time daily outdoors, and, like St. Thérèse, thinking about God. I believe that the beauty, the rhythm, the flow, and the openness of poetry lends itself particularly useful as we journey closer to God with our beloved children and grandchildren in union with what Pope Frances calls "the joyful mystery of God" in creation. May God bless you!

16 July, 2019, Feast of Our Lady of Mount Carmel

A Few Explanations and Suggestions
The Purpose of This Study

The purpose of this poetical study of nature through the seasons is two-fold:

1) To seek and experience God personally and intimately by daily exposure to His creative work in nature

2) To better appreciate the connection between all of God's creation, its meaning and value, and its role—and ours—in the harmonious praise of God

Briefly, each creation of God has its own value and significance as well as a unique nature that is dependent on the rest of creation. Each creature works to complete and serve the rest of creation. (See *CCC* ¶340.) All of creation's natures, working together as a system of natures, are what we call "nature"—which "can only be understood as a gift from the outstretched hand of the Father of all" (*Laudato Si'* ¶76). The purpose of all of God's creation—including us—is to give Him praise and glory: ". . . so that we might exist for the praise of his glory . . ." (Ephesians 1:12).

Our study of God's creation through poetry and outdoor exploration is intended to allow children—and their adult companions—to experience God in a different way, to see Him in a new light, and to deepen our relationship and appreciation for Him and all of His creation—to learn to pray and praise God continuously. This is not a new way of experiencing God. Check out the Psalms and other books of the Bible. Refer to the writings of St. Thomas

1

Aquinas and many other saints. Peruse the teachings of our last three popes—St. Pope John Paul II, Pope Benedict XVI, and Pope Francis. Read through the *Catechism of the Catholic Church*, which clearly states: "There is a solidarity among all creatures arising from the fact that all have the same Creator and are all ordered to his glory . . ." (344). (For a more thorough treatment of seeking God through nature in accordance with the teachings of the Catholic Church, please see the Appendix of this book.)

Hopefully, through the gentle art of poetry and a daily commitment to experience God's creation outdoors, our relationship with God will become more awestruck as it becomes filled with the wonder, love, and appreciation of His divine wisdom and loving providence. God is more than willing to meet us whenever we reach out to Him. A little bit of openness and availability on our part will go a long way toward helping us fulfill our mission to praise God's glory in all our being. Let us begin today.

How this Study Is Organized

Astronomical vs. Meteorological Seasons

Astronomical seasons are based on where the sun is in relation to the Earth, with the equinoxes (March and September) marking the dates where the day-to-night ratio is exactly twelve hours each. Because the Earth does not take exactly 365 days to travel around the sun, these dates vary but are generally considered to be March 21 and September 22 with the solstices usually falling on June 21 and December 22—the days with the longest and shortest periods of daylight. So the first day of each season according to the astronomical calendar would correspond to the varying dates of the spring and fall equinoxes and the summer and winter solstices.

The meteorological calendar for seasons uses the more general three-month chunk of time that is most closely associated with that season's weather. This calendar has the following seasonal dates:

- Winter: December 1 to February 28 or 29
- Spring: March 1 to May 31
- Summer: June 1 to August 31, and
- Autumn: September 1 to November 30

As the meteorological seasonal calendar corresponds more closely with our liturgical year, which begins in the season of Advent around December 1, (and breaks the months of each season more cleanly), this poetical study of the seasons uses the meteorological calendar to track the seasons.

(Please note that much of the material in this study is geared toward the weather and activities common to the temperate climates. My personal experience is almost exclusively that of the upper Midwest of the United States. Adaptation may be necessary depending on your location.)

LITURGICAL VS. NATURAL YEAR

Traditionally, we Americans often begin new projects and make new resolutions at the beginning of our Gregorian calendar year on January 1. Our Church's Roman Rite liturgical new year always begins on the first Sunday of Advent. This date is determined by when the Sunday closest to the Feast of St. Andrew (November 30) falls. The earliest this date can be is November 27, and the latest possible date is December 3. The beginning of the winter season of this series would roughly correspond with the beginning of the Church's liturgical new year.

The other major season of the liturgical year is the season of Lent, which is generally associated with the natural

3

season of spring. As the timing of this season depends on the moveable feast day of Easter, Ash Wednesday, the first day of Lent, may be as early as February 4 or as late as March 10, with the date of Easter itself ranging from March 22 to April 25. Therefore, the Lenten season is covered in this study in both the winter and spring seasons.

WHEN AND HOW TO START

There is no "right" starting place for this series—no "correct" season to begin this poetical study of God's creation. Many may wish to start with the Church's new liturgical year in December—the winter season. However, feel free to start with the season that best suits your own calendar and availability. Perhaps summer, when school is in recess and life is more laid back, is a better fit for your schedule. Quite possibly, autumn— the beginning of the school year—appeals to you as the best time to start. Maybe you want to examine the optional theme for each season and choose to begin according to which theme seems most interesting to you and your family.

Whenever you begin, remember the program's two main rules:

1. Read one poem daily *aloud* and have a short discussion on it. (Suggestions for age-appropriate questions can be found below.)
2. Spend at least thirty minutes each and every day outdoors, exploring God's beautiful creative work. This includes you as well as the children. Always keep in mind that the best way to get children outdoors is to go with them. Trust me; you will be enriched beyond your expectations. Do not hesitate to assume the role of nature mentor to help

4

your children or grandchildren increase their love of nature and deepen their experience of God. Review the section on nature mentoring if you need the reassurance that no prior experience or knowledge is necessary. You—yes, you—can do this!

THE DAILY ROUTINE

THE POEMS – DAILY AND SUPPLEMENTAL

For each day of the year, a poem (or several shorter poems) is presented for reading. The poem may be about an aspect of nature for that season, relate to the seasonal theme, or to a specific activity common for that season. Read each poem aloud. Perhaps each child could also read the poem aloud. Read slowly and with feeling. Don't hesitate to re-read the poem several times. If a child takes a special liking to a poem, help the child to memorize it. Having three or four favorite poems in a memory bank provides a store of great pleasure that will bubble up and spill out on days when our love of nature overwhelms us and we have no other way to express our joy in that special experience. It is a great treasure.

In addition to the daily poems, several other poems are available in the supplemental poetry section following the daily poems. These poems focus on the liturgical year or specific national holidays. They may be chosen to read aloud instead of, or in addition to, the poem for each day. There is a poem available for each day of Christmas, each day of Lent, and at least one poem for each significant holiday or Catholic holy day. Additionally, there are poems for meditation upon the themes for the First Friday and First Saturday devotions. Use the supplemental poems as you deem best for your family— either replacing the daily poem, read in addition to the daily poem, or not read at all. If you wish to incorporate them into the daily routine, it may require some preparation time to preview these poems to determine which ones best suit your family and purposes. Be sure to discuss these poems with the children/grandchildren just as you would the daily poems.

As you and your family begin to read more and more poetry, be sure to note favorite poets. Go online and check out more poems by these favorites or perhaps purchase as a gift an entire volume written by them. Pay attention to the type of poetry (rhythm and rhyme scheme) that appeals to each child. Encourage them to take a favorite poem, study how it is written, and use it as a pattern for writing an original poem of their own. Perhaps after reading a poem, they may decide that they could write a better poem on that topic. The world needs poetry and poets; coax the young poets around you to produce poetry that they enjoy writing and sharing. Model writing poetry by generating poems of your own.

DISCUSSION

To encourage discussion, always ask open-ended questions that require more than a yes/no answer. For younger children, the following questions offer a good beginning but remember that not all questions will apply to every poem. As you gain confidence, feel free to construct your own questions geared toward the ages and interests of your own children/grandchildren.

1. What is this poem about?
2. How does this poem make you feel?
3. What action do you want to take because of this poem?
4. What did you learn from this poem?
3. What does this poem suggest about God?

A different approach is to ask each child to retell the poem in their own words, starting with the youngest child and having each child add something to the re-telling. (Educator Charlotte Mason calls this technique "narration.")

For older children (and adults), try using the following three principles/realities/values that stem from the teachings of Thomas Berry, Catholic eco-theologian and author of several books including *The Dream of the Earth* and *The Great Work: Our Way into the Future*. According to Thomas Berry, these three characteristics govern the universe and reveal what the universe has to teach us. (These questions are also appropriate to ask as a nature mentor when outside exploring nature with children.)

1. Uniqueness (Each creation offers a unique expression of the divine, an authenticity that illustrates how the divine image dwells within.)
   - How is this creation different from all others? What makes it unique?
   - How does it reveal the divine?

2. Interior Identity
   - What is the job or specific task of this creation?
   - How does it function?
   - How does it give harmonious praise to God?

3. Communion/Connection
   - What is the relationship between this creation and the rest of creation?
   - How does it serve or provide for the rest of creation?
   - How is it connected to or dependent upon the rest of creation?

THE QUOTATIONS

The quotations beneath the daily poems are included for the adults participating in this study. Often, as we feed our children the knowledge and inspiration they crave and need, our own needs may go unfulfilled. These short selections are intended to inspire you, deepen your understanding about an idea or topic, or add a touch of humor.

ADDITIONAL RESOURCES

This section first includes appropriate picture books for children. In preparation for this section, hundreds of possibly worthy picture books were read and examined; many of these books were discarded in favor of the exceptional books chosen for each season. The books marked "Stellar" would be considered "must reads" for each season. The remaining books have been categorized according to the holidays and optional themes for each season. The intention is that these books would be read aloud by either an adult or child.

Depending on the interests of your children/grandchildren, you may wish to focus on one particular theme or perhaps choose several books from each category. (It would be hard to read them all!) As you read through these books, be sure to note the author of those books you particularly enjoy. Watch for other books by these authors listed in this series, and/or check them out at your local library.

After the final section of picture books, there is a short section on other nature books for children. This section varies with the season and is outlined below.

Summer: A Short List of Children's Nature Poets, Collectable Children's Poetry Books, and A Few Children's Poetry Anthologies

Fall: A Short List of Children's Nature Chapter Books
Winter: Nature Non-fiction Books for Children
Spring: A Short List of Children's Nature Authors

The last part of this section contains recommended adult books that fall loosely in the following categories:

- The "Why" of Nature
- Connection with Nature
- Nature Activity Books—Outdoor Adventuring
- Nature Journaling
- Nature Crafts and Drawing Books
- Nature Books for Grandparents
- The Practice of *Shinrin-yoku:* Forest Therapy or Forest Bathing
- The Practice of Mindfulness

OUTSIDE ACTIVITY

The crux and primary purpose of this poetry series is to explore nature and to seek God in His beautiful creation. If you are unsure about what to do outside, check out the "Additional Resources" section described above for ideas. Assume your role as nature mentor as described on pages 17-21 below.

By spending unfettered time in nature, we will unleash our sense of wonder and come to better understand God. By increasing our familiarity with different aspects of nature, we will begin to see the connection between all creation and discover the loving concern God has for His creation.

Please make the effort to get your family (including yourself!) outside for least thirty minutes each day—an hour would not be too much! Get outside, play, experience creation, and live in the present moment. Be sure to pause occasionally in holy silence to give thanks, glory, and praise to our awesome Creator!

OPTIONAL SEASONAL THEMES

For those interested in a more guided study of nature, each season has a theme of recommended focus. These themes provide a hub around which outside activity for each season can be centered as well as an emphasis on specific knowledge and experience of God's created world.

Do not get obsessive with the suggested resources below. Choose only those best suited to your particular situation. Be flexible. Taylor these suggestions to your own circumstances and time allowances.

SUMMER THEME: Inspecting God's Glorious Creation through Naming Nature (Nomenclature)

- DEFINITION OF NOMENCLATURE: A system of names in a given field such as botany or biology

- GOAL: Naturalist—someone who is an expert or student in the study of plants, animals, and the natural world

- SUMMARY: By taking an interest in nature and being willing to make the acquaintance of the most common natural elements in your locale—by learning the names of the most common birds, flowers, and trees—we can become more acquainted with all that surrounds us in God's great outdoors. Names foster familiarity, and lead to a sense of connection. "What I know of the divine sciences and the Holy Scriptures, I have learned in woods and fields. I have no other masters than the beeches and the oaks" (St. Bernard of Clairvaux).

- ADULT RESOURCES
  - *Beyond Your Doorstep* by Hal Borland
  - *Circle of the Seasons* by Edwin Way Teale

📖 *Exploring Nature with Your Child* by Dorothy Edwards Shuttlesworth

📖 *Great Lakes Nature* by Mary Blocksma

📖 *Handbook of Nature Study* by Anna Botsford Comstock [a classic since 1939]

📖 *The Naturalist's Notebook* by Nathaniel T. Wheelwright and Bernd Heinrich

- CHILDREN'S RESOURCES

  📖 Regional field guides (the more specific to your area the better) to birds, flowers, insects, trees, or any other area of interest

  📖 *Nature Anatomy* by Julia Rothman

  📖 Any of the *True Books* (*True Book of Insects*, etc.) published by Children's Press in the 1950's and 1960's

  📖 Any of Jim Arnosky's *Crinkleroot's Guide to Knowing* books (*Birds*, *Trees*, etc.)

  📖 *Crinkleroot's Guide to Walking in Wild Places*

AUTUMN THEME: Respecting God's Creation through Care of the Natural World

- GOAL: Eco-Catholic

- DEFINITION OF ECO-CATHOLIC: Someone who values not only Catholic spirituality and doctrine but also the natural world, the environment, and justice

- SUMMARY: In his 2015 encyclical *Laudato Si'*, Pope Francis encourages "every person living on this planet" to take better care of our common home, Earth. Like his three predecessors, he emphasizes the need to care for and understand the connection between all of God's creation. Review carefully your family's relationship with the natural world and the habits that support the environment and those that are detrimental. "Care for the environment represents a challenge for all of humanity. It is a matter of a common and universal duty, that of respecting a common good" (Pope St. John Paul II, *Centesimus Annus*, 40).

- ADULT RESOURCES
  - 📖 *Caring for Creation in Your Own Backyard: Over 100 Things Christian Families Can Do to Help the Earth (A Seasonal Guide)* by Loren & Mary Ruth Wilkinson
  - 📖 *Earthsongs: Praying with Nature* by Wayne Simsic
  - 📖 *In Defense of Nature* by Benjamin Wiker
  - 📖 *Laudato Si'* by Pope Francis
  - 📖 *Life from Our Land* by Marcus Grodi
  - 📖 *The Joyful Mystery: Field Notes toward a Green Thomism* by Christopher J. Thompson

- CHILDREN'S RESOURCES
  - 📖 *Celebrate the Earth: Psalm 104* by Dorrie Papademetriou
  - 📖 *Crinkleroot's Guide to Giving Back to Nature* by Jim Arnosky
  - 📖 *Song of Francis* by Tomie dePaola
  - 📖 Read and implement actions proposed by Pope Francis in ¶211 of *Laudato Si'*.

WINTER THEME: Reflecting on the Mystery of God through Natural Prayer

- DEFINITION OF NATURAL PRAYER: Finding intimacy with God by experiencing Him in the beauty of nature; prayer experienced amidst creation (Beware, however, of the caution expressed by St. John of the Cross in *Ascent of Mount Carmel* 3.24.4: If the heart and soul are not elevated to

God, an experience of sensory delight may merely be another form of recreation.)

- GOAL: Mystic—someone who seeks union with God through prayer and self-surrender
- SUMMARY: The season of winter—when much of nature is at rest and we anticipate and contemplate the Mystery of God in the Christ Child—is a great time to reconnect with that wonder for God that natural experiences (a beautiful sunset, a snowy-topped mountain, a perfect snowflake) so easily enkindle. Enjoy the stillness of winter while practicing the virtue of holy silence—quiet walks in the snow, a pause to listen to the winter birds. Take your daily prayer time (rosary or meditation) outside. "We need to find God, and he cannot be found in noise and restlessness. God is the friend of silence. See how nature—trees, flowers, grass—grows in silence; see the stars, the moon and the sun, how they move in silence . . ." (St. Teresa of Calcutta).

- ADULT RESOURCES
  - *Natural Prayer: Encountering God in Nature* by Wayne Simsic
  - *The Secret Life of John Paul II* by Lino Zani
  - *When the Trees Say Nothing* by Thomas Merton

- CHILDREN'S RESOURCES
  - *A Quiet Place* by Douglas Wood
  - *Crinkleroot's Book of Animal Tracking* by Jim Arnosky
  - *The Other Way to Listen* by Byrd Baylor
  - *The Wild Weather Book* by Fiona Danks and Jo Schofield

SPRING THEME: Detecting God in Nature through Phenology

- DEFINITION OF PHENOLOGY: Nature's calendar; nature's clock; the study of the timing of seasonal biological activities including first flowers, leaf budding, bird migration, etc. (We can also include *seasonality*, which is the study of changes in the physical environment such as first frost, date the ice melts, etc.)

- GOAL: Nature Detective—someone who carefully observes the wonders and mystery of nature

- SUMMARY: Spend spring observing firsts and lasts in nature: first robin, first eruptions of various plants and flowers, first sound of the frog voices, last frost, last ice on the lake. Mark these dates on a regular or perpetual calendar—an excellent beginning toward keeping a more complete nature journal. Allow the children free rein to explore and take notes and photos of various aspects of God's creation. "Nature is a constant source of wonder and awe" (Pope Francis, *Laudato Si'* 85).

- ADULT RESOURCES
  - Daily readings from any of the following: *Hal Borland's Book of Days* (New England), *A Walk through the Year* by Edwin Way Teale (New England), or *Wit & Wisdom of the Great Out-doors* by Larry Wilber (upper Midwest)
  - Or weekly readings from *The Beginning Naturalist* by Gale Lawrence or shorter articles for each month in *A Seasonal Guide to the Natural Year* by John Bates

(upper Midwest), or *Minnesota Phenology* by Larry Weber
- 📖 **Or** browse through any calendar/almanac suited to your location.
- 📖 Check into joining a citizen science program of interest.

- CHILDREN'S RESOURCES
  - 📖 *Crinkleroot's Nature Almanac* by Jim Arnosky
  - 📖 *One Day in the Woods* by Jean Craighead George
  - 📖 *This World of Wonder* by Hal Borland
  - 📖 *When I Consider* by Marian M. Schoolland

Note that these suggested themes are *optional*. If the children are young, or if the themes seem intimidating to implement, feel free to skip them. Perhaps you would like to utilize the picture books as your only use of the optional season themes. Or maybe you would like to study the suggested adult resources for your own enrichment without adding the children's resources.

Be kind to yourself. We're going for joy here—not added stress! Do not put pressure to use every resource and/or theme. Attach no guilt to customizing and simplifying. The main objective is to enjoy God's creation and to connect with the Creator—not to cram in every possible teaching moment. Allow the children to ask and find answers to their own spontaneous questions in an adventure of discovery at their own lead. Relax and enjoy!

"FOR FROM THE GREATNESS
AND THE BEAUTY OF CREATED THINGS
THEIR ORIGINAL AUTHOR,
BY ANALOGY,
IS SEEN."

WISDOM 13:5

YOU CAN BECOME A NATURE MENTOR
(ALMOST WITHOUT TRYING)

"If a child is to keep alive his inborn sense of wonder . . . he needs the companionship of at least one adult who can share it, rediscovering with him the joy, excitement, and mystery of the world we live in" (Rachel Carson in *A Sense of Wonder*). This "one adult" becomes this child's nature mentor. It is not a difficult task. It does not require vast knowledge. According to Rachel Carson, it is based upon "having fun together rather than teaching." Whether you are a grandparent, a parent, a teacher, the neighbor down the street, or an aunt like Rachel Carson, you need no advance preparation other than asking yourself, "Am I up for adventure?" "Can I handle being a co-conspirator?"

The best nature mentors are not those who have the answers but who can stimulate the questions, who can step aside and let the child take charge. Effective nature mentors are those who are fellow adventurers, willing to let their own sense of wonder come alive, and share their feelings about nature—and reverence for nature—rather than merely providing explanations and facts. Observe and explore. Be aware and listen—not only to the wonders around you but to those sharing the experience with you. Be respectful to the child's interests and enthusiasms. Be attentive to the present moment—the activity and the feelings that are evoked.

Ask questions. Point out interesting sights, sounds, animals, and plants. Bring home specimens to talk about, learn about, and display. Include God in the discussion.

Help them to observe the activity around them. Allow them to directly experience the wonder that surrounds them —saving the "teaching moment" for a later recap of the event. Encourage them to see, hear, smell, and touch. Allow them not only to run and enjoy but also to sit in holy silence and observe—watch the grass bending in the wind, hear the babble of nearby water and birds, smell the flowers and the bark of the trees, touch the moss and slippery rocks—pondering and raising the heart to God. The love of nature is best inspired by experiencing nature —even quiet observation can be an interactive encounter on an emotional level.

Be enthusiastic and joyful in all their discoveries. Play games; join in their fun. Often, the memory of an experience is associated with the emotions related to that experience. By making time with nature joy-filled, joy will come to be an emotion associated with nature itself.

Sharing the natural world with others adds to the richness of the encounter—not only at the moment but later in discussion. Take time each day to reflect together on time spent in nature, reviewing individual discoveries and emotions. In this way, everyone benefits from each person's experience and insights, and our own encounters become more meaningful. Additionally, a bit of nature bonding and affirmation occurs that binds us with each other, and more deeply with the created world.

As a nature mentor, basic knowledge may be helpful but, in this case, only a little knowledge of nature is not a dangerous thing—or even detrimental. Enjoyment of simple natural aspects (the colors of the sunset, the blowing clouds, the calls of birds, the vastness of the night sky, the feel of rain on your face) will serve to enkindle more joy and wonder than many interesting facts. "I sincerely believe that for the child, and for the parent seeking to guide him, it is not half so important to know as to feel" (Rachel Carson).

It is more helpful to arouse their curiosity and sense of wonder than to pepper them with facts and names they may or may not be able to assimilate. As a nature mentor, receptivity and awareness trump personal resources. Is it less wondrous to gaze at the night sky even if you do not know the name of a single star or constellation?

Encourage exploration using the senses of smell and hearing. This is particularly effective at night and in rainy weather. The smell of the ocean, frog ponds, and rain-filled forests can provide lasting memories. The night sound of insects, frogs, flight of birds overhead, thunder, and wind are especially powerful. Try to focus not only on the full chorus of sound but also on each of the individual contributors. Seek where they are hiding.

Unfortunately, it is easy to become immune to the wonder of God's creation—to become insensitive to repeated exposure to God's great gifts. Rachel Carson would have us ask, "What if I had never seen this before? What if I knew I would never see it again?" Like the reception of Holy Communion, when we take for granted that we can receive It often, we often receive It less (and less reverently). The same holds true of God's gifts within the natural world. Because we can see it all the time, we often see (and enjoy its benefits) less often. When is the last time you took the time to explore the night sky? Or pause your busy agenda to enjoy the glorious sunset? Or listen attentively for even a minute or two to the morning chorus of birds? Learn to tune in to God not only in church, but also in His cathedral of the natural world.

RESOURCES

So what resources are required to be an effective nature mentor? For starters, you may want to read one or more of the books that most directly influenced the above insights and ideas:

📖 *The Sense of Wonder* by Rachel Carson (1956)

📖 *Sharing Nature with Children: The Classic Parents' and Teachers' Nature Awareness Guidebook* by Joseph Cornell (1979—a newer edition is available)

📖 *How to Raise a Wild Child: The Art and Science of Falling in Love with Nature* by Scott D. Sampson (2015)

Spending a few dollars on a good magnifying glass or hands lens will pay off handsomely. With this, a snowflake or grain of sand takes on far greater wonder as does a drop of pond water or the moon at night. You may wish to throw down another couple of dollars on child-sized flashlights—or ultraviolet flashlights!—for night exploration of insects, rocks, and flowers. (Bedtime can wait!)

As far as expensive equipment and toys, do not let your heart be troubled. In 2012, *Wired* magazine published an article entitled "The 5 Best Toys of All Time." Here is your shopping list:

1. Stick
2. Box
3. String
4. Cardboard Tube
5. Dirt

If you must spend money, a few good field guides may be helpful—the more regional the better—for identification of common trees, birds, flowers, and insects. Keep in mind, however, this caution from Rachel Carson: "I think the value of the game of identification depends on how you play it. If it becomes an end in itself, I count it of little use. It is possible to compile extensive lists of creatures seen and identified without ever once having caught a breath-taking glimpse of the wonder of life. If a child asked me a question that suggested even a faint awareness of the mystery behind the arrival of a migrant sandpiper on the beach of an August morning, I would be far more pleased than by the mere fact that he knew it was a sandpiper and not a plover."

A pair of puddle boots, some old clothes, and raingear (purchased or makeshift) will allow your child to explore without fear of "getting dirty." Be sure to provide the same for yourself.

Nature mentoring really is as simple as accompanying kids outside and letting them do what comes naturally. Let them be the boss. If you are doubtful, try at least a half-hour outside every day for a month—put it on your calendar. While Scott Sampson in *How to Raise a Wild Child* claims, "The best place to fall in love with nature is wherever you happen to be," be sure to vary the setting occasionally. Find a place where you (as well as the children) are excited to be. See what effect this daily thirty-minute habit has—on you and the kids!

Rachel Carson had one wish for every child: ". . . a sense of wonder so indestructible that it would last throughout life, as an unfailing antidote against the boredom and disenchantments of later years, the sterile preoccupation with things that are artificial, the alienation from the sources of our strength." It is in wonder that we often find God.

"... HE FIXED THE ORDERED SEASONS
AND THE BOUNDARIES OF
THEIR REGIONS,
SO THAT PEOPLE MIGHT SEEK GOD,
EVEN PERHAPS GROPE FOR HIM
AND FIND HIM,
THOUGH INDEED HE IS NOT FAR
FROM ANY ONE OF US."

ACTS 17:26-27

JUNE

GOD'S WORLD
Published in the
"Altoona Tribune", June 11, 1931

I'm glad I am living this morning
Because the day is so fair,
And I feel God's presence so keenly
About me, everywhere.

The heavens declare His glory,
The trees seem to speak of His power,
And I see His matchless beauty
In each small, growing flower.

The rocks all tell of His wonder;
In the hills His strength I see;
And the birds are singing His praises
In the songs that they sing to me.

Oh, I'm glad to be living this morning
In a world of beauty so rare
Where the God of Heaven is hovering
About me, everywhere.

> "So the **LORD** God formed out of the ground all the wild animals and all the birds of the air, and he brought them to the man to see what he would call them; whatever the man called each living creature was then its name."
>
> Genesis 2:19

JUNE

Douglas Malloch (1877-1938), published in
The Melody of Earth, 1918

I knew that you were coming, June, I knew that you
were coming!
Among the alders by the stream I heard a partridge
drumming;
I heard a partridge drumming, June, a welcome with his
wings,
And felt a softness in the air half Summer's and half
Spring's.

I knew that you were nearing, June, I knew that you
were nearing—
I saw it in the bursting buds of roses in the clearing;
The roses in the clearing, June, were blushing pink and
red,
For they had heard upon the hills the echo of your
tread.

I knew that you were coming, June, I knew that you
were coming,
For ev'ry warbler in the wood a song of joy was
humming.
I know that you are here, June, I know that you are
here—
The fairy month, the merry month, the laughter of the
year!

"I understood that if all flowers wanted to be roses,
nature would lose her springtime beauty, and the
fields would no longer be decked out with little wild
flowers." – St. Therese of Lisieux

SONG OF SUMMER
Maud L. Betts, published in
Child-Garden of Story, Song and Play, 1894

Jack Frost and the Winter have gone far away,
    And good-bye we have said to the Spring;
But Summer has come, with her sweet smiling
    face,
        All her blossoms and treasures to bring.

She has drest all the fields in robes of soft green,
    With daisy and buttercup trimming;
And her every hour, each day that she stays,
    Is with laughter and light o'erbrimming.

Dear Summer, we love you, and wish you would
    stay,
        And yet, when the cool Autumn is here,
We'll love her as much, for we cannot but love,
        Every season which come in the year.

"Why must people kneel down to pray? If I really
wanted to pray I'll tell you what I'd do. I'd go out into
a great big field all alone or into the deep, deep
woods, and I'd look up into the sky—up- up- up- into
that lovely blue sky that looks as if there was no end
to its blueness. And then I'd just feel a prayer . . ."
Anne in *Anne of Green Gables* by L. M. Montgomery)

FLOWERS ARE SPRINGING
Matthias Barr (1831-1931), published in
The Child's Garland of Little Poems, 1866

Flowers are springing,
Birds are singing,
Bees are humming all around;
Joy and pleasure,
Without measure,
Welcome you in every sound.

In the meadows,
Lights and shadows
Chase each other far away.
Lambs are bleating,
Swallows fleeting;
All this happy summer's day!

"The power to classify, discriminate, distinguish
between things that differ is amongst the highest
faculties of the human intellect, and no opportunity
to cultivate it should be let slip; but classification got
out of books, that the child does not make for himself
and is not able to verify for himself, cultivates no
power but that of verbal memory."
Charlotte Mason

SONG OF SUMMER
Mary Mapes Dodge (1831-1905), published in
Bancroft's First-Fifth Reader: Book 3, 1883

Up in the treetop, down in the ground,
High in the blue sky, far, all around,
Nearby, and everywhere, creatures are living:
God, in His bounty, something is giving.

Up in the tree top, down in the ground,
High in the blue sky, far, all around,
Nearby, and everywhere, creatures are striving;
Labor is surely the price of their thriving.

Up in the tree top, down in the ground,
High in the blue sky, far, all around,
Nearby, and everywhere, singing and humming,
Busily, joyfully, summer is coming!

HOSPITALITY
John Bannister Tabb (1845-1909), published in
Child Verse, 1900

Said a Snake to a Frog with a wrinkled skin,
"As I notice, dear, that your dress is thin,
And a *rain* is coming, I'll take you in."

"Almost all children have a natural love of living
creatures, and if they are told interesting facts about
them they soon become ardent naturalists."
Elizabeth Brightwen

CLOUDS
Christina Rossetti (1830-1894), published in
Sing Song, A Nursery Rhyme Book, 1872

White sheep, white sheep
On a blue hill.
When the wind stops
You all stand still.

You walk far away
When the winds blow;
White sheep, white sheep,
Where do you go?

"Forget not that the earth delights to feel your bare
feet and the winds long to play with your hair."
Kahlil Gibran

St. Norbert

Robert Hugh Benson (1871-1914), published in
An Alphabet of Saints, 1906

"**N**" for ST. NORBERT, a man of Cologne,

Who was friends with the Emperor then on the throne;
He lived the gay life of a courtier—I mean
He was not quite so good as he ought to have been.
He was hunting one day, when a thunderbolt fell
And reminded this courtier of Judgment and Hell.
Resolving that he would be worldly no more,
He sold his possessions to give to the poor,
And set out like a sower to sow the good seed
In a land overgrown with heretical weed.
A number of people abandoned the world
To serve under the banner St. NORBERT unfurled;
For our LADY designed him a habit of white
(Like the ANGELS') and *Showed* him a *Meadow*, the site
Where, in loving accord with our LADY'S intentions,
He built the first House of the Premonstratensians.

(ST. NORBERT, Bishop and Confessor, Founder, A.D. 1119, of the Premonstratensians [*Pré montré* means "Meadow shown"], or White Canons, sometimes called Norbertines; Born at Cologne, 1065; Died, May 6, 1134. Feast, June 6)

"Jesus said to him, 'If you wish to be perfect, go, sell what you have and give to [the] poor, and you will have treasure in heaven. Then come, follow me.'"
Matthew 19:21

ALONE

John Chipman Farrar (1896-1974), published in
Forgotten Shrines, 1919

White daisies are down in the meadow,
And queer little beetles and things,
And sometimes nice rabbits and field mice
And blackbirds with red on their wings.

I want to explore all alone,
With nobody spying around,
All alone, all alone, all alone!
It has such a wonderful sound. . . .

"We are trying to open the books of nature to
children by the proper key—knowledge,
acquaintance by look and name, if not more, with
bird, and flower and tree. . ." – Charlotte Mason

THE BEST THING
(FROM "EVA'S VISIT TO FAIRYLAND")
Louisa May Alcott (1832-1888), published in
"Lulu's Library: Volume 2, 1887

"I shine," says the sun,
"To give the world light,"
"I glimmer," adds the moon,
"To beautify the night."
"I ripple," says the brook,
"I whisper," sighs the breeze,
"I patter," laughs the rain,
"We rustle," call the trees.
"We dance," nod the daisies,
"I twinkle," shines the star,
"We sing," chant the birds,
"How happy we all are!"
"I smile," cries the child,
Gentle, good, and gay;
The sweetest thing of all,
The sunshine of each day.

"The sun does not shine for a few trees and flowers,
but for the wide world's joy." – Henry Ward Beecher

DANDELION

Nellie M. Garabrant, published in *Nature in Verse:
A Poetry Reader for Children*, 1895

There's a dandy little fellow,
Who dresses all in yellow,
In yellow with an overcoat of green;
With his hair all crisp and curly,
In the springtime bright and early
A-tripping o'er the meadow he is seen.
Through all the bright June weather,
Like a jolly little tramp,
He wanders o'er the hillside, down the road;
Around his yellow feather,
Thy gypsy fireflies camp;
His companions are the wood lark and the toad.

But at last this little fellow
Doffs his dainty coat of yellow,
And very feebly totters o'er the green;
For he very old is growing
And with hair all white and flowing,
A-nodding in the sunlight he is seen.
Oh, poor dandy, once so spandy*,
Golden dancer on the lea**!
Older growing, white hair flowing,
Poor little baldhead dandy now is he!

* neat; complete

** pasture; prairie

"The love of nature is a different thing from the love of
science, though the two may go together."
John Burroughs

BOATS SAIL ON THE RIVERS
Christina Rossetti (1830-1894), published in
Sing Song, A Nursery Rhyme Book, 1872

Boats sail on the rivers,
  And ships sail on the seas;
But clouds that sail across the sky
  Are prettier far than these.

There are bridges on the rivers,
  As pretty as you please;
But the bow that bridges heaven,
  And overtops the trees,
And builds a road from earth to sky,
  Is prettier far than these.

"The heavens declare the glory of God;
the firmament proclaims the works of his hands."
Psalms 19:2

RAINDROPS
Ellen Walsh, published in *Religious Poems for Little Folks*, 1936

Q*uestion*
Little drops of water,
Sparkling in the sun,
Tell us, tiny raindrops,
What work have you done?

Answer
We kissed the blushing rose
Needing drink so long;
We greeted little birds
Who gladdened you by song.

Dropping on the hillside,
Made the grasses green,
Freshened all the flowers;
What a sight was seen!

Little sister raindrops,
Worked in brook and rill*,
Sparkled in the sunshine,
Turned for flour the mill.

We say low to nature,
When we kiss the sod,
"We are busy workers
Sent to you from God."

* very small stream

"Let them [children] once get touch with Nature, and a habit is formed which will be a source of delight through life. We were all meant to be naturalists, each in his degree, and it is inexcusable to live in a world so full of the marvels of plant and animal life and to care for none of these things."
Charlotte Mason

THE VIOLET
Jane Taylor (1783-1824), published in
Little Ann and Other Poems, 1883

Down in a green and shady bed,
    A modest violet grew,
Its stalk was bent, it hung its head,
    As if to hide from view.

And yet it was a lovely flower,
    Its colors bright and fair;
It might have graced a rosy bower,
    Instead of hiding there,

Yet there it was content to bloom,
    In modest tints arrayed;
And there diffused its sweet perfume,
    Within the silent shade.

Then let me to the valley go,
    This pretty flower to see;
That I may also learn to grow
    In sweet humility.

"It seems to me that if a little flower could speak, it would tell simply what God has done for it without trying to hide its blessings." – St. Therese of Lisieux

St. Antony of Padua

Robert Hugh Benson (1871-1914), published in
An Alphabet of Saints, 1906

"**A**" is ANTONY of PADUA, a Friar wise and
   kind;
He never had a penny, but he never seemed to mind;
He was very fond of reading, but the book he read
   the most
Was the book that tells of GOD, the Father, Son
   and Holy Ghost;
He was very fond of children, but the Child he loved
   the best
Was the little Infant JESUS, as He lay on Mary's
   breast;
And once when he was reading with the Gospel on
   a stand
Little JESUS stood upon it and caressed him with
   His hand.
      Now that ANTONY'S in Heaven, if you
            ever lose your toys,
      I advise you to invoke him, for he's good
            to girls and boys.

(ST. ANTONY of PADUA, Confessor, Friar Minor of the
Order of Saint Francis of Assisi. Born in Portugal, 1196;
Died at Padua, 1231. Feast, June 13)

"They who keep holy the things that are holy shall
themselves become holy." – Abraham Heschel

June 14

THE FLAG OF OUR COUNTRY
Published in *American Cardinal Reader: Book 2,* 1929

O, this is the flag of our country,
The flag of red, white, and blue.
The red says, "Be brave!"
The white says, "Be pure!"
The blue tells us to be true.

OUR FLAG
Mary Howlister, published in *Happy Holidays,* 1921

There are many flags in many lands,
There are flags of ev'ry hue,
But there is no flag in any land,
Like our own Red, White, and Blue. . . .

Then "Hurrah for the Flag!" our country's flag,
Its stripes and white stars, too.
There is no flag in any land,
Like our own Red, White and Blue.

"The American flag doesn't give her glory on a
peaceful, calm day. It's when the winds pick up and
become boisterous, do we see her strength."
Anthony Liccione

June 15

THE KING'S HIGHWAY
Rt. Rev. Hugh F. Blunt (1877-1957), published in
Ideal Catholic Readers: Second Reader, 1915

I saw her walking through the field,
   God's mother with her Son,
And every little flower-bell pealed
   To praise the Holy One.

Oh, every little rose upturned
   To wave as He did pass,
And every little sunbeam burned
   Its incense on the grass!

Oh, every little piping bird
   Did trumpet from the tree,
And every little lambkin heard,
   And danced, God's Lamb to see!

Oh, Nature all did serenade
   God's mother and her Son;
And then I knew why God had made
   His creatures—every one!

"I only went out for a walk and finally concluded to
stay out till sundown, for going out, I found,
was really going in." – John Muir

DUSK IN JUNE
Sara Teasdale (1884-1933), published in
Rivers to the Sea, 1915

Evening, and all the birds
In a chorus of shimmering sound
Are easing their hearts of joy
     For miles around.

The air is blue and sweet,
The few first stars are white,
Oh, let me like the birds
     Sing before night.

BE LIKE THE BIRD
Victor Hugo (1802-1885), published in *The Critic,*
Volume 4, 1885

Be like the bird that, halting in her flight
Awhile, on boughs too slight,
Feels them give way beneath her and yet sings.
Knowing that she has wings.

"These people have learned not from books, but in
the fields, in the wood, on the river bank. Their
teachers have been the birds themselves, when they
sang to them, the sun when it left a glow of crimson
behind it at setting, the very trees, and wild herbs."
Anton Chekhov, *A Day in the Country*

TIT FOR TAT

Christopher Morley (1890-1957), published in
Chimneysmoke, 1921

I often pass a gracious tree
Whose name I can't identify,
But still I bow, in courtesy
It waves a bough, in kind reply.

I do not know your name, O tree
(Are you a hemlock or a pine?)
But why should that embarrass me?
Quite probably you don't know mine.

"Even rain and wind and stormy clouds bring joy, just
as knowing animals and flowers and where they live."
Sigurd F. Olson

DAISES

Frank Dempster Sherman (1860-1916), published in
The Poems of Frank Dempster Sherman, 1887

At evening when I go to bed
I see the stars shine overhead;
They are the little daisies white
That dot the meadow of the night.

And often while I'm dreaming so,
Across the sky the Moon will go;
It is a lady, sweet and fair,
Who comes to gather daisies there.

For, when at morning I arise,
There's not a star left in the skies;
She's picked them all and dropped them down
Into the meadows of the town.

DAISIES

Christina Rossetti (1830-1894), published in *Sing Song, A Nursery Rhyme Book,* 1872

Where innocent bright-eyes daisies are,
With blades of grass between,
Each daisy stands up like a star
Out of a sky of green.

". . . Just as in nature all the seasons are arranged in such a way as to make the humblest daisy bloom on a set day, in the same way everything works out for the good of each soul." – St. Therese of Lisieux

FOUR-LEAF CLOVER

Ella Higginson (1861-1940), published in
When the Birds Go North Again, 1898

I know a place where the sun is like gold
And the cherry blooms burst with snow,
And down underneath is the loveliest nook
Where the four-leaf clovers grow.

One leaf is for hope, and one is for faith,
And one is for love, you know,
And God put another one in for luck;
If you search, you will find where they grow.

But you must have hope, and you must have faith,
You must love and be strong, and so
If you work, if you wait, you will find the place
Where the four-leaf clovers grow.

"The beauty of creation is one of the fundamental
tutors in the faith and points us to the reality of God
and His Presence in a compelling way."
Christopher J. Thompson, *The Joyful Mystery*

MERRY SUNSHINE
Eleanor Smith, published in
"Bulletin: Bureau of Education", 1919

"Good morning, Merry Sunshine,

How did you wake so soon?
You've scared the little stars away
And driven away the moon.

I saw you go to sleep last night
Before I ceased my playing;
How did you get 'way over there,
And where have you been staying?"

"I never go to sleep, dear child,
I just go round to see
My little children of the East,
Who rise and watch for me.

I waken all the birds and bees
And flowers on my way,
And last of all the little child
Who stayed out late to play."

TIME TO RISE
Robert Louis Stevenson (1850-1894), published in
A Child's Garden of Verses, 1913

A BIRDIE with a yellow bill

Hopped upon the window sill,
Cocked his shining eye and said:
"Ain't you 'shamed, you sleepy-head!"

"All I have seen teaches me to trust the Creator for all
I have not seen." – Ralph Waldo Emerson

June 21
St. Aloysius Gonzaga

SAINT ALOYSIUS

Sister Mary Josita Belger (1899-1978), published in
Sing a Song of Holy Things, 1945

Aloysius was a rich, young boy.
He might have been a king,
But he gave his money all away;
He did not keep a thing.

He went to Rome to be a priest,
To honor Jesus' Name.
He left his parents and his friends.
To serve his God he came.

His soul was like a pure, white flower
That blooms in sunny May—
A lily of the valley sweet,
You see along the way.

He did not ever in his life
Commit a mortal sin.
But in his thoughts and words and deeds
He tried God's love to win.

When his short life was ended
All heaven was filled with joy.
The little saints and angels ran
To meet this holy boy.

"I refuse to yield this body to its earth without having
done all I can, with the help of His grace, to give glory
and honor to the One who has fashioned us all."
Christopher J. Thompson, *The Joyful Mystery*

BED IN SUMMER

Robert Louis Stevenson (1850-1894), published in
A Child's Garden of Verses, 1885

In winter I get up at night
And dress by yellow candle-light.
In summer, quite the other way,
I have to go to bed by day.

I have to go to bed and see
The birds still hopping on the tree,
Or hear the grown-up people's feet
Still going past me in the street.

And does it not seem hard to you,
When all the sky is clear and blue,
And I should like so much to play,
To have to go to bed by day?

"'Come to me, all you who labor and are burdened,
and I will give you rest.'" – Matthew 11:28

A FEW OF THE BIRD-FAMILY

James Whitcomb Riley (1849-1916), published in
*The Complete Works of James Whitcomb Riley:
Volume 4*, 1913

The old bob white, and chipbird;
> The flicker and chee-wink,
> And little hopty-skip bird
> Along the river brink.

The blackbird and snowbird,
> The chicken-hawk and crane;
> The glossy old black crow-bird,
> And buzzard, down the lane.

The yellowbird and redbird,
> The tom-tit and the cat;
> The thrush and that redhead bird
> The rest's all pickin' at!

The jay-bird and the bluebird,
> The sap-suck and the wren
> The cockadoodle-doo bird,
> And our old settin' hen!

"Sociologists point out that American kids today can identify a thousand corporate logos but less than ten native plants and animals that live around their homes."
William Powers, *Twelve by Twelve*

NATURE

Kate Louise Brown (1837-1921), published in
The Plant Baby and Its Friends, 1899

O Nature! Loving Nature!
The mother-side of God,
We see thy faithful tending
Where'er our feet have trod.

There's mystery in every seed,
And glory in the flower;
The meanest glassblade speaks of Thee,
Thy tenderness and power.

So we go on not knowing,
Thy glory veils our sight.
The child-heart and the child's deep faith
Will guide the soul aright.

"I like to think of nature as an unlimited broadcasting station, through which God speaks to us every hour, if we only tune in." – George Washington Carver

RAINING

Amelia Josephine Burr (1878-1968), published in
The Bellman Book of Verse, 1919

Raining, raining,
All night long;
Sometimes loud, sometimes soft,
Just like a song.
There'll be rivers in the gutters
And lakes along the street.
It will make our lazy kitty
Wash his little dirty feet.
The roses will wear diamonds
Like kings and queens at court;
But the pansies all get muddy
Because they are so short.
I'll sail my boat tomorrow
In wonderful new places,
But first I'll take my watering-pot
And wash the pansies' faces.

"How beautiful is the rain!
After the dust and heat,
In the broad and fiery street,
In the narrow lane,
How beautiful is the rain!"
Henry Wadsworth Longfellow

THE SECRET
Arthur Wallace Peach (1886-1956), published in
The Melody of Earth, 1918

O, little bird, you sing
As if all months were June;
Pray tell me ere you go
The secret of your tune?

"I have no hidden word
To tell, nor mystic art;
I only know I sing
The song within my heart!"

OVERHEARD IN AN ORCHARD
Elizabeth Cheney
published in *Record of Christian Work*, 1921

Said the robin to the sparrow,
"I should really like to know
Why these anxious human beings
rush about and worry so."

Said the sparrow to the robin,
"Friend, I think that it must be
That they have no Heavenly Father
Such as cares for you and me."

"Those who contemplate the beauty of the earth find
reserves of strength that will endure as long as life
lasts." – Rachel Carson

THE LOON

Lew Sarett (1888-1954) published in
Anthology of Magazine Verse, 1920

A lonely lake, a lonely shore,
A lone pine leaning on the moon,
All night the water-beating wings
Of a solitary loon.

With mournful wail from dusk to dawn,
He gibbered at the taunting stars—
A hermit-soul gone raving mad
And beating at his bars.

"I thought about Mom. She craved silence more than anyone I know. And not just the kind of silence you get when you sit inside and turn off the television and phone. That kind of silence often feels lonely and hollow. The silence that Mom craved was far from silent. It's what she got when you listen to it, you don't feel alone. You feel like you're a part of something infinitely bigger than yourself." – Mark Woods, *Lassoing the Sun*

SOME ONE

Walter De La Mare (1873-1956), published in *Collected Poems: 1901-1980, Songs from Childhood*, 1920

Some one came knocking
At my wee, small door;
Some one came knocking
I'm sure—sure—sure;
I listened, I opened,
I looked to left and right,
But nought there was a-stirring
In the still dark night;
Only the busy beetle
Tap-tapping in the wall,
Only from the forest
The screech-owl's call,
Only the cricket whistling
While the dewdrops fall,
So I know not who came knocking,
At all, at all, at all.

"The silence rings—it is musical & thrills me. A night in which the silence was audible—I hear the unspeakable." – Henry David Thoreau

TREES
Sara Coleridge (1802-1852), published in
Pretty Lessons in Verse for Good Children, 1839

The Oak is called the king of trees,
The Aspen quivers in the breeze,
The Poplar grows up straight and tall,
The Peach tree spreads along the wall,
The Sycamore gives pleasant shade,
The Willow droops in watery glade,
The Fir tree useful in timber gives,
The Beech amid the forest lives.

THE FIVE-FINGERED MAPLE
Kate Louise Brown (1837- 1921), published in
The Journal of Education: Volume 87, 1918

"Green leaves, what are you doing
Up there on the tree so high?"
"We are shaking hands with the breezes
As they go singing by."

"What, green leaves! Have you fingers?"
Then the Maple laughed with glee.
"Yes, just as many as you have;
Count us and you will see."

"I took a walk in the woods and came out
taller than the trees." – Ralph Waldo Emerson

HOW LARGE THE WORLD (CONTEMPLATION)
John Alden Carpenter (1876-1951), published in
Improving Songs for Anxious Children, 1913

For days and days I've climbed a tree,
   A dappled yellow tree,
And gazed abroad at many things
   I've always wished to see.

I see the green and gentle fields
   All bounded in with hedge,
And shining river swimming through
   The rushes on his edge.

And little sheep who play all day,
   I watch them as they run,
While far away the roofs of town
   Are shining in the sun.

I think it's very nice to sit
   So high and look so far.
How very large the world can be!
   How many things there are!

"The more I study nature, the more amazed I am at
the work of the Creator." – Louis Pasteur

JULY

JULY
Susan Hartley Swett (1860-1907), published in
A Year of Beautiful Thoughts, 1902

When the scarlet cardinal tells
Her dream to the dragonfly,
And the lazy breeze makes a nest in the trees,
And murmurs a lullaby,
It is July.

When the tangled cobweb pulls
The cornflower's cap awry,
And the lilies tall lean over the wall
To bow to the butterfly,
It is July.

When the heat like a mist veil floats,
And poppies flame in the rye,
And the silver note in the streamlet's throat
Has softened almost to a sigh,
It is July.

When the hours are so still that time
Forgets them, and lets them lie
'neath petals pink till the night stars wink
At the sunset in the sky.
It is July.

"LIFT UP YOUR EYES ON HIGH AND SEE WHO CREATED* THESE: HE LEADS OUT THEIR ARMY AND NUMBERS THEM, CALLING THEM ALL BY NAME. . . ." – ISAIAH 40:26

A BIG PLAYFELLOW
Published in *A Jolly Jingle-Book*, 1913

It's lots of fun down in the grass,
A-watching all the things that pass!
You won't come too? I wonder why
It's fun a-playing with the sky!

I guess you are too tall to see;
If you would come down here with me,
And just *ungrow* a little, you
Could see just what you wanted to.

Such big cloud-ships with sails spread out
To catch the breeze that's all about!
And big gray birds with soft cloud-wings,
And wolves and bears and tiger things!

Just lying down here in the grass,
I've seen about a million pass;
They creep and run and sail and fly—
It's fun a-playing with the sky!

"The soul can split the sky in two, and let the face of
God shine through. – Edna St Vincent Millay

THE COUNTRY FAITH
Norman Gale (1862-1942), published in
A Country Muse, 1893

Here in the country's heart
   Where the grass is green,
   Life is the same sweet life
   As it e'er hath been.

Trust in a God still lives,
   And the bell at morn
Floats with a thought of God
   O'er the rising corn.

God comes down in the rain,
   And the crop grows tall—
This is the country faith,
   And the best of all.

"Sometimes I am worried by the thought of the effect
that life in the city will have on coming generations."
John Burroughs

THE FLAG GOES BY
Henry Holcomb Bennett (1795-1894), published in
War Readings, 1918

Hats off!

Along the street there comes
A blare of bugles, a ruffle of drums,
A flash of color beneath the sky.
Hats off!
The flag is passing by!

Blue and crimson and white it shines,
Over the steel-tipped, ordered lines.
Hats off!
The colors before us fly;
But more than the flag is passing by.

Sea-fights and land-fights, grim and great,
Fought to make and to save the State:
Weary marches and sinking ships;
Cheers of victory on dying lips . . .

Sign of a nation, great and strong
Toward her people from foreign wrong:
Pride and glory and honor,—all
Live in the colors to stand or fall.

Hats off!
Along the street there comes
A blare of bugles, a ruffle of drums,
And loyal hearts are beating high:
Hats off!
The flag is passing by!

"Upon his will he binds a radiant chain,
for Freedom's sake he is no longer free."
Joyce Kilmer

FOURTH OF JULY

James J. Metcalfe (1906-1960), published in
Poems for Children, 1950

Today is Independence Day,
And everybody cheers
While fireworks of every kind
Are bursting in our ears.

The big parade is on its way;
Our flag is held up high
As soldiers, sailors and marines
Go proudly marching by.

It is the day we set aside
To celebrate our birth,
And all that we have done for peace
And freedom on this earth.

"What can you do to promote world peace? Go
home, and love your family." – St. Teresa of Calcutta

Picnic

James J. Metcalfe (1906-1960), published in
Poems for Children, 1950

A picnic is the thing to have
When summer comes around,
And we can spread the tablecloth
And food upon the ground.

The chance to fill our tummies in
A quiet country nook,
And play a game of softball or
Go wading in the brook.

A picnic is a paradise
Of fun for one and all—
Unless there are too many ants,
Or rain begins to fall.

"It's not enough to be busy; so are the ants. The
question is, what are you busy about?"
Henry David Thoreau

IN THE GARDEN
Emily Dickinson (1830-1886), published in
The Poems of Emily Dickinson, Series Two, 1896

A bird came down the walk:
He did not know I saw;
He bit an angle-worm in halves
And ate the fellow, raw.

And then he drank a dew
From a convenient grass,
And then hopped sidewise to the wall
To let a beetle pass.

CATERPILLAR
Christina Rossetti (1830-1894), published in
Sing Song, A Nursery Rhyme Book, 1872

Brown and furry
Caterpillar in a hurry,
Take your walk
To the shady leaf, or stalk.

May no toad spy you,
May the little birds pass by you;
Spin and die,
To live again a butterfly.

"Here, on this patch of earth, I either love the Lord
and keep His earth or I don't." – Christopher J.
Thompson, *The Joyful Mystery*

THE DAISY
Sir Rennell Rood (1858-1941), published in
The Progressive Music Series, 1914

With little white leaves in the grasses,
Spread wide for the smile of the sun,
It waits till the daylight passes,
Then closes them one by one.

I have asked why it closed at even,
And I know what it wished to say:
"There are stars all night in the heaven,
And I am the star of the day."

"The day was made for laziness; and lying on one's
back in green places, and staring at the sky till its
brightness forced one to shut one's eyes and go to
sleep." – Charles Dickens

FIREFLY

Elizabeth Madox Roberts (1881-1941), published
in *Under the Tree*, 1922

A little light is going by,
　Is going up to see the sky,
A little light with wings.

I never could have thought of it,
　To have a little bug all lit
And made to go on wings.

LOVELY THINGS
Sister M. Noel, published in
Song of the Rood, 1940

I shall remember lovely things:

The thrilling joy when a bluebird wings
Its way through the dusk of eventide
To a quiet tree on the mountain side;
The dainty flit of a butterfly;
The delicate blue of a drifting sky;
The silent call of the evening star;
The rose's perfume wafted* far.
I shall remember lovely things:
A smile, a tear, a heart that sings.

* drifted; floated

"'From panoramic vistas to the tiniest living form,
nature is a constant source of wonder and awe. It is
also a continuing revelation of the divine.'"
Canadian Bishops, quoted in *Laudato Si'* 85

DANDELION, WHAT DO YOU DO?
Published in *School Education:*
Volume 19, 1900

"O dandelion, yellow as gold,
What do you do all day?"

"I just wait here in the tall green grass
Till the children come out to play."

"O dandelion, yellow as gold,
What do you do all night?"

"I wait and wait till the cold dews fall
And my hair grows long and white."

"And what do you do when your hair is white
And the children come out to play?"

"They take me up in their dimpled hands,
And blow my hair away."

"Each creature, Thomas [Aquinas] affirms, bears the impress of the divine and seeks, however feeble its powers, to manifest His glory to the best of its ability."
Christopher J. Thompson, *The Joyful Mystery*

ST. BENEDICT

Robert Hugh Benson (1871-1914), published in
An Alphabet of Saints, 1906

Before ST. BENEDICT, Hermit and Sage,
Whose Rule has been kept by most Monks since his age.
Cyrilla, his Governess, took him from home
To learn how to read at a day-school in Rome,
Where he went to his lessons with satchel and pen,
And rode back by the Tiber to supper again.
He loved contemplation so much that one day
He agreed with Cyrilla to run right away;
And for years in the mountains he fasted and prayed
Till the praise of the neighbors made BENET afraid;
So he wandered and wandered, but stayed in the end
In a cave near ROMANUS the Monk, his good friend.
Before long many Monks gathered round him to pray,
And his Rule and his Monks are still mighty today.

O Blessed St. BENET, I wish I could be
Half as good for one year as you were sixty-three.

(ST. BENEDICT, Abbot, Patriarch of all Western
Monks, Founder of the Order called Benedictine; Born at
Nursia, in Italy, 480; Died at Monte Cassino, 543)

". . . The days will come when the bridegroom is taken
away from them, and then they will fast."
Matthew 9:15

DUCKS DITTY
Kenneth Grahame (1859-1932), published in
The Wind in the Willows, 1908

All along the backwater,
　　Through the rushes tall,
Ducks are a-dabbling.
　　　Up tails all!

Ducks' tails, drakes' tails,
　　Yellow feet a-quiver,
Yellow bills all out of sight
　　　Busy in the river!

Slushy green undergrowth
　　Where the roaches swim
Here we keep our larder*,
　　　Cool and full and dim.

Every one for what he likes!
　　We like to be
Head down, tails up,
　　　Dabbling free!

High in the blue above
　　Swifts whirl and call
We are down a-dabbling
　　　Up tails all!

* a pantry or cupboard for food

"No man ever steps in the same river twice, for it's not
the same river and he's not the same man."
Heraclitus

FOREIGN LANDS

Robert Louis Stevenson (1850-1894), published in
A Child's Garden of Verses, 1885

Up into the cherry tree
   Who should climb but little me?
I held the trunk with both my hands
   And looked abroad in foreign lands.

I saw the next door garden lie,
   Adorned with flowers, before my eye,
And many pleasant places more
   That I had never seen before.

I saw the dimpling river pass
   And be the sky's blue looking-glass;
The dusty roads go up and down
   With people tramping in to town.

If I could find a higher tree
   Farther and farther I should see,
To where the grown-up river slips
   Into the sea among the ships,

To where the road on either hand
   Lead onward into fairy land,
Where all the children dine at five,
   And all the playthings come alive.

"In music, in the sea, in a flower, in a leaf, in an act of
kindness . . . I see . . . God in all these things."
Pablo Casals

THE SWING

Daniel A. Lord (1888-1955), published in
Chants for Children, 1942

Up we go and down we drop,
Swinging so high, and a sickening stop.
Up to the birds' nests hidden in leaves,
Touching the edge of the house's eaves.
　　Down and up; up and down;
　　Frown and smile, smile and frown.

Why, when we're up, can't we stay up there?
Why do we drop, with a rush of air?
Once you are high, the earth seems flat,
Daddy has told me that life's like that.
　　Down and up; up and down;
　　Frown and smile, smile and frown.

Up from the earth till we touch the skies,
Knock at the portals of Paradise.
Someday we'll swing from the earthly sod
Up to the welcoming arms of God.
　　Always up; never down;
　　Always smile; never frown.

"You are never too old to play outside."
Janet McKenzie

TREES

Joyce Kilmer (1886-1918), published in
Trees and Other Poems, 1914

I think that I shall never see
A poem as lovely as a tree.

A tree whose hungry mouth is pressed
Against the earth's sweet flowing breast;

A tree that looks at God all day,
and lifts her leafy arms to pray;

A tree that may in Summer wear
A nest of robins in her hair;

Upon whose bosom snow has lain;
Who intimately lives with rain.

Poems are made by fools like me,
But only God can make a tree.

"We are the poetry of God." – See Ephesians 2:10

FLOWER OF CARMEL (FLOS CARMELI)
St. Simon Stock (1164-1265)

Flower of Carmel,
Tall vine blossom laden;
Splendor of heaven,
Childbearing yet maiden.
None equals thee.

Mother so tender,
Whom no man did know,
On Carmel's children
Your favors bestow.
Star of the Sea. . . .

O gentle Mother
Who in Carmel reigns,
Share with your servants
That gladness you gained
and now enjoy.

Hail, Gate of Heaven,
With glory now crowned,
Bring us to safety
Where your Son is found,
true joy to see.

"Joy is the serious business of heaven." – C. S. Lewis

OUTDOOR LIFE

Helen Emma Maring (1900-19??), published in
Anthology of Newspaper Verse for 1922

Outdoor life's a wondrous thing
　　When poets all about it sing.

It's nice to read about in books,
　　And all right as to outward looks.
In real life, it is a fright,
　　With mice and bats abroad at night,
With caterpillars, snakes, and slugs,
　　A million different kinds of bugs
Including spiders, ants, and flies,
　　And lady-bugs with staring eyes.

Mean threatening wasps and buzzing bees
　　Play havoc with a fellow's ease,
The beaches are alive for fair
　　With sand-fleas hopping everywhere,
With crabs that crawl, and clams that squirt,
　　And skeeter bugs that bite and hurt.
This outdoor life is surely fine,
　　But quiet city days for mine.

"Yet even the supposedly useless—mosquitoes,
leeches, spiders, snakes, rats and vultures—all have
their place in God's creation and show the amazing
intricacy of His miraculous and providential
creativity." – Marcus Grodi, *Life on Our Land*

THE LESSON
(FROM "THE TOWN CHILD AND THE COUNTRY CHILD")
Allan Cunningham (1784-1842), published in
Selections from the British Poets, 1851

There is a lesson in each flower,
    A story in each stream and bower;
In every herb o'er which you tread,
    Are written words, which, rightly read,
Will lead you, from earth's fragrant sod,
    To hope, and holiness, and God.

"Naturalists, like poets, are born and then made only
by years of painstaking observation." – John Burroughs

A Rainy Day Plan

Nancy Byrd Turner (1880-1971), published in
In Play Land, 1911

The world's wet and stormy,
    The wind's in a rage.
We are shut in the house
    Like poor birds in a cage.
There's a sigh in the chimney,
    A roar on the wall.
Good-by to "I Spy"
    And to swinging and all!
But the child that complains
    Cannot better the day,
So the harder it rains,
    Why, the harder we'll play!

There are tears on the window
    And sighs in the trees,
But who's going to fret
    Over matters like these?
If the sky's got to cry,
    Then it's better by half
That the longer it weeps,
    Why, the louder we'll laugh!
And look! I declare,
    There's the sun coming out
To see what on earth
    All the fun is about!

"The startled storm-clouds reared on high
And plunged in terror down the sky."
Edna St. Vincent Millay, "Renascence"

SEA SHELL

Amy Lowell (1874-1925), published in
Dome of Many-Coloured Glass, 1912

Sea Shell, Sea Shell,

Sing me a song, O Please!
A song of ships, and sailor men,
And parrots, and tropical trees,
Of islands lost in the Spanish Main
Which no man ever may find again,
Of fishes and corals under the waves,
And seahorses stabled in great green caves.
Sea Shell, Sea Shell,
Sing of the things you know so well.

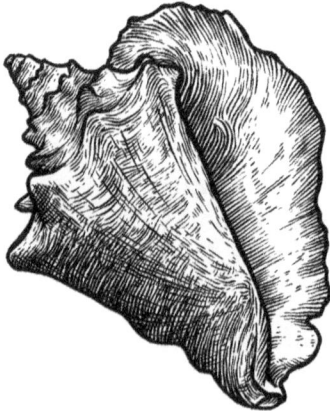

"The sea, once it casts its spell, holds you in the net of
its wonder." – Jacues Cousteau

AT THE SEA-SIDE
Robert Louis Stevenson (1850-1894), published in
A Child's Garden of Verses, 1885

When I was down beside the sea
A wooden spade they gave to me
To dig the sandy shore.

My holes were empty like a cup.
In every hole the sea came up,
Till it could come no more.

FISHES
Published in *Introduction to
Waldorf Education*, 1979

Freckled fishes, flirting, flitting,
Flashing fast or floating free,
Flicking filmy fins like feathers,
Feeding from the floating sea.

"There is a pleasure in the pathless woods, There is a
rapture on the lonely shore, There is society, where
none intrudes, By the deep sea, and music in its roar: I
love not man the less, but Nature more." – Lord Byron

GOD AND THE SEA
Daniel A. Lord (1888-1955), published in
Chants for Children, 1942

God must be very like the sea,
As vast and strong as He can be.
He holds me safely when I swim,
And likes it when I play near Him.

He's very angry when I'm bad,
Yet never hurt His little lad.
Someday I'll cross the ocean blue
And see, dear God, the rest of you.

"Live in the sunshine. Swim in the sea.
Drink the wild air." – Ralph Waldo Emerson

THE BUTTERBEAN TENT
Elizabeth Madox Roberts (1881-1941),
published in *Under the Tree*, 1922

All through the garden I went and went,
And I walked in under the butterbean tent.

The poles leaned up like a good tepee
And made a nice little house for me.

I had a hard brown clod for a seat,
And all outside was a cool green street.

A little green worm and a butterfly
And a cricket-like thing that could hop went by.

Hidden away there were flocks and flocks
Of bugs that could go like little clocks.

Such a good day it was when I spent
A long, long while in the butterbean tent.

"The kiss of the sun for pardon
The song of the birds for mirth,
One is nearer God's Heart in a garden
Than anywhere else on earth."
Dorothy Frances Gurney

HOW DOTH THE LITTLE BUSY BEE
Isaac Watts (1674-1748), published in
Dr. Watts' Divine & Moral Songs, 1806

How doth the little busy bee
Improve each shining hour,
And gather honey all the day
From every opening flower!

How skillfully she builds her cell!
How neat she spreads the wax!
And labors hard to store it well
With the sweet food she makes.

In works of labor or of skill,
I would be busy too;
For Satan finds some mischief still
For idle hands to do.

In books, or work, or healthful play,
Let my first years be passed,
That I may give for every day
Some good account at last.

THE SONG OF THE BEE
Old Jingle

Buzz-zz, Buzz-zz, Buzz-zz!
This is the song of the bee.
His legs are all yellow,
This jolly good fellow,
A very hard worker is he!

"Never be inside when you could be outside. Spend most of the first six years of life outside."
Charlotte Mason

ST. CHRISTOPHER
[ADAPTED]
Rev. John B. Tabb (1845-1909)

It was a very little Boy
That on the river side
Stood calling, "Ferryman, ahoy!
Come, take me o'er the tide!"

The Ferryman came wading on,
And seeing but a child,
"Get up upon my shoulder, Son,"
He said, and, stooping, smiled.

But when into the stream again
The giant boldly strode,
His every muscle was astrain
Beneath the growing load;

Till finally, with failing strength,
He reached the other bank,
And putting down the Boy, at length
Upon the margin sank.

"Who are you," wondering, he cried,
"That has so burdened me?"
"The Son of God," the Boy replied,
"Who bore the Cross for thee.

"Henceforth your task pursuing here
For love of souls forlorn
You'll bear the name of Christopher,
As you the Christ has borne;

"And little sufferers that see
How great is your reward
Shall cry, 'like Christopher are we
Your Ferrymen, O Lord.'"

"Bear one another's burdens, and so you will fulfill the
law of Christ." – Galatians 6:2

July 26
St. Joachim and St. Anne

O GOOD SAINTE ANNE
[ADAPTED]
Old Breton Sailor Hymn

We sailors who travel the roads of the sea
Find safety and calm when we call upon thee.

Sainte Anne, we implore you to hark to our prayer,
In time of our danger, take us in your care.

O good Sainte Anne, we call on your name,
Your praise and your glory your children proclaim.

"I never go down a city street when the dusk is falling,
but I think of small boats going out to sea."
Harold Vinal

THE BEES AND THE SPIDER
Matthias Barr, published in
The Child's Garland of Little Poems, 1866

A hive stood under a garden tree,
'Mid all that was lovely and fair to see,
And far and near, in meadow and bower,
The bees went humming from flower to flower.

A spider watched them with eyes of hate,
Watched them early and watched them late,
And he spun him a web and said with a smile,
"Pray lend me your company, neighbors, a while."

But the bees were too busy, the livelong day,
To heed what the spider had to say,
They wrought* and wrought and went to their rest
With the golden sun in the crimson west.

Young reader, a moral you may discern:,
Never be idle when you may learn,
But work, work, work, like the busy bee,
And no evil web shall entangle thee.

* work

"Nearly every season, I make the acquaintance of
one or more new flowers." – John Burroughs

THE FRIENDLY TREE

Mary Mabel Wirries (1893-1967), published in
Gay Witch April and Other Poems, 1936

There's a queer old tree on the avenue,
Hunchbacked, and crooked as it can be.
It talks to me when I walk along
And when I'm past, it waves at me.

I love it best, though it looks queer;
The trees that are straight and fine and high,
Don't even notice a child like me—
They just keep looking at the sky

But the nice old crooked, homely tree
Bends down low. It's my *friendly* tree.
I whisper to it, when I go by:
"I'm awfully glad you wave at me."

"Time spent amongst trees is never wasted time."
Katrina Mayer

THE KATYDIDS

James Whitcomb Riley (1849-1916), published in
Joyful Poems for Children, 1902

Sometimes I keep
From going to sleep,
To hear the katydids "cheep-cheep!"
And think they say
Their prayers that way;
But katydids don't have to pray!

I listen when
They cheep again
And so, I think, they're singing then!
But, no; I'm wrong,—
The sound's too long
And all-alike to be a song!
I think, "Well, there!
I do declare,
If it is neither song nor prayer,
It's talk—and quite
Too vain and light
For me to listen to all night!"

And so, I smile,
And think—"Now I'll
Not listen for a little while!"—
Then, sweet and clear,
Next "cheep" I hear
'S a kiss . . . Good morning, Mommy dear!

"That I may praise God's name in song
and glorify it with thanksgiving." – Psalms 69:31

THE CHERRY TREE
Bjorrstjerne Bjornson (1832-1910), published in
Songs of the Tree-Top and Meadow, 1899

The trees' early leaf buds were bursting their brown;
"Shall I take them away?" said the frost, sweeping down.
"No, leave them alone
Till the blossoms have grown,"
Prayed the tree, while she trembled from rootlet to
    crown.

The tree bore her blossoms, and all the birds sung:
"Shall I take them away?" said the wind, as he swung:
"No, leave them alone
Till the blossoms have grown,"
Said the tree, while his leaflets quivering hung.

The tree bore her fruit in the midsummer glow:
Said the child, "May I gather the cherries now?"
"Yes, all you can see;
Take them; all are for thee,"
Said the tree, while she bent down her laden boughs
    low.

"All nature smelt of the opulent summer time, smelt of
the season of fruit." – Theocritus

ST. IGNATIUS

Robert Hugh Benson (1871-1914), published in
An Alphabet of Saints, 1906

"I" for IGNATIUS, a brave Spanish Knight,
Who was wounded and had to retire from the fight;
He asked for a book that would answer his needs,
Some book about battles and chivalrous deeds,
But they gave him the Lives of the Saints, which he
read
From beginning to end as he lay ill in bed;
And when he had finished, he vowed and he swore
That he'd follow the Saints and be worldly no more.

No longer a soldier, he rose from his bed
And enlisted an Army for JESUS instead.

(ST. Ignatius of Loyola, Confessor, Founder of the
Society of Jesus, or Jesuits; Born at Loyola, Spain, 1491;
Died in Rome, 1556)

"Do not love the world or the things of the world. If
anyone loves the world, the love of the Father is not in
him." – 1 John 2:15

AUGUST

AN OUTDOOR GIRL
Published in *A Jolly Jingle-Book*, 1913

The wind and the water and a merry little girl—
Her yellow hair a-blowing and her curls all out of
  curl,
Her lips as red as cherries and her cheeks like any
  rose,
And she laughs to see the little waves come curling
  round her toes.
The breezes a-blowing and the blue sky overhead,
A laughing little maiden—and this is what she
  said:
"Oh, what's the use of houses? I think it is a sin
To take a lot of boards and bricks and shut the
  outdoors in!"

> "I WRITE OF FLOWERS, BUT NATURE IS EVIDENCED IN SEASCAPES AND MOUNTAINTOPS, MAJESTIC TREES, FLORA AND FAUNA."
> ST. POPE JOHN PAUL II

THE CHILD'S WORLD
William Brighty Rands (1823-1882), published in
Child's Calendar Beautiful, 1906

Great, wide, beautiful, wonderful World
With the wonderful water around you curled,
And the wonderful grass upon your breast,
World, you are beautifully dressed.

The wonderful air is over me,
And the wonderful wind is shaking the tree;
It walks on the water, and whirls the mills,
And talks to itself on the top of the hills.

You friendly Earth, how far do you go
With the wheat fields that nod, and the rivers that
flow,
With cities and gardens and cliffs and isles,
And people upon you for thousands of miles?

Ah! You are so great, and I am so small,
I tremble to think of you, World, at all;
And yet, when I said my prayers today,
A whisper inside of me seemed to say:

"You are more than the Earth, though you are
such a dot.
You can love and think, and the Earth cannot."

"We were not meant to be inundated by cement,
asphalt, glass and metal, and deprived of physical
contact with nature." – *Laudato Si'* 44

THE SWING
Robert Louis Stevenson (1850-1894), published in
A Child's Garden of Verses, 1885

How do you like to go up in a swing,
   Up in the air so blue?
Oh, I do think it the pleasantest thing
   Ever a child can do!

   Up in the air and over the wall,
      Till I can see so wide,
   Rivers and trees and cattle and all
      Over the countryside—

   Till I look down on the garden green,
      Down on the roof so brown—
   Up in the air I go flying again,
      Up in the air and down!

"Look deep into nature, and you will understand
everything better." – Albert Einstein

The Eagle
Alfred, Lord Tennyson (1809-1892),
first published in 1851

He clasps the crag with crooked hands;
Close to the sun in lonely lands,
Ring'd with the azure* world, he stands.

The wrinkled sea beneath him crawls;
He watches from his mountain walls,
And like a thunderbolt he falls.

* bright blue

"The eagle is a bird of large ideas; he embraces long distances; the continent is his home." – John Burroughs

August 4

THE SELFISH SEA
Mary Carolyn Davies (1888-1940?), published in
A Little Freckled Person, 1919

The sea is very, very wide;

It takes up all the room outside;
And when I stand beside the sea,
It comes right up and pushes me!

"Never will I forget the impression the sea made upon
me; I couldn't take my eyes off it since its majesty, the
roaring of its waves, everything spoke to my soul of
God's grandeur and power." – St. Therese of Lisieux

ALONG THE BEACH
Daniel A. Lord (1888-1955), published in
Chants for Children, 1942

I love to play upon the sand
And pull the seaweed with my hand,
And gather shells of every kind.
You ought to see the ones I find.

I love to watch the gulls at play,
Like zooming planes they swoop and sway.
For tiny fish I love to dip,
Or find the wreckage of a ship.

I'll bet the strangest things must lie
Where sea comes up and meets the sky.
I'll bet that's where sea serpents roam,
And fairies have their island home.

God must have tossed this sand around
To make my happy playing ground.
I'll bet when Jesus was like me
He loved to play beside the sea.

"Everybody needs beauty as well as bread, places to play in and pray in, where nature may heal and give strength to body and soul." – John Muir

IT'S GOOD, LORD, TO BE HERE [ADAPTED]

Joseph A. Robinson (1858-1933), published in
Hymns Ancient and Modern, 1904

It's good, Lord, to be here,
Your glory fills the night;
Your face and garments, like the sun,
Shine with unborrowed light.

It's good, Lord, to be here,
Your beauty to behold,
Where Moses and Elijah stand,
Your messengers of old.

Fulfiller of the past,
Promise of things to be,
We hail Your body glorified,
And our redemption see.

Before we taste of death,
We see Your kingdom come;
Before us keep Your vision bright,
And make this hill our home.

It's good, Lord, to be here,
yet we may not remain;
But since You bid us leave the mount,
Come with us to the plain.

"And he was transfigured before them; his face shone
like the sun and his clothes became white as light.
And behold, Moses and Elijah appeared to them,
conversing with him." – Matthew 17:2-3

MY SHADOW

Robert Louis Stevenson (1850-1894), published in
A Child's Garden of Verses, 1885

I have a little shadow that goes in and out with me,
And what can be the use of him is more than I can see.
He is very, very like me from the heels up to the head;
And I see him jump before me, when I jump into my bed.
The funniest thing about him is the way he likes to grow—
Not at all like proper children, which is always very slow;
For he sometimes shoots up taller like an India-rubber
    ball,
And he sometimes gets so little that there's none of him
    at all.
He hasn't got a notion of how children ought to play,
And can only make a fool of me in every sort of way.
He stays so close behind me, he's a coward you can see;
I'd think shame to stick to nursie as that shadow sticks
    to me!
One morning, very early, before the sun was up,
I rose and found the shining dew on every buttercup;
But my lazy little shadow, like an arrant* sleepy-head,
Had stayed at home behind me and was fast asleep in
    bed.

* complete; total

"Most of the shadows of this life are caused by our
standing in our own sunshine." – Ralph Waldo Emerson

August 8
St. Dominic

St. Dominic

Robert Hugh Benson (1871-1914), published in
An Alphabet of Saints, 1906

"**D**" for ST. DOMINIC, Spanish by birth,
Who shone like a star in all parts of the earth.
In France there were heretics called Albigenses
Who poisoned the Faith with their lying pretences,
And spread their ridiculous nonsense about;
But St. DOMINIC went and soon hunted them out.
Then with Lawrence and Bertrand and Peter Cellani
He started his Order of Dominicani,
Or *Domini Canes*, the Dogs of the LORD,
Who go hunting for souls in the might of the Word.
The MASTER they follow in black-and-white coat
To catch men by the heart instead of the throat.
    Our LADY much loved this dear Knight of the LORD,
    And her Rosary served for his Buckler and Sword.

(ST. DOMINIC, Confessor, Founder of the Order of
Preachers, or Preaching Friars; called in Latin
Dominicani after him [*Domini Canes* is Latin for
"Hounds of the Lord"]; Born in Spain, 1170; Died at
Bologna, in Italy, August 6, 1111. Feast, August 8)

"He said to them, 'Come after me, and I will make
you fishers of men.'" – Matthew 4:19

THE LITTLE TURTLE
Vachel Lindsay (1879-1931), published in
The Golden Whales of California, 1920

There was a little turtle.
He lived in a box.
He swam in a puddle.
He climbed on the rocks.

He snapped at a mosquito.
He snapped at a flea.
He snapped at a minnow.
And he snapped at me.

He caught the mosquito.
He caught the flea.
He caught the minnow.
But he didn't catch me.

"If I am not I, who will be?" – Henry David Thoreau

AUGUST HEAT
Published in *Read-Aloud Rhymes for the Very Young*,
1986

In August, when the days are hot,

I like to find a shady spot,

And hardly move a single bit—

And sit—

    And sit—

        And sit—

            And sit.

"'To sit in the shade on a fine day, and look upon
verdure is the most perfect refreshment.'"
Jane Austen, *Mansfield Park*

August 11

ON THE BRIDGE

Kate Greenaway (1846-1901), published in
Marigold Garden, 1885

If I could see a little fish—
That is what I just now wish!
I want to see his great round eyes
Always open in surprise.

I wish a water-rat would glide
Slowly to the other side;
Or a dancing spider sit
On the yellow flags a bit.
I think I'll get some stones to throw,
And watch the pretty circles show.
Or shall we sail a flower boat,
And watch it slowly—slowly float?
That's nice—because you never know
How far away it means to go;
And when tomorrow comes, you see,
It may be in the great wide sea.

"Life is fast, and I've found it's easy to confuse the
miraculous for the mundane so I'm slowing down,
way down in order to give my full presence to the
extraordinary that infuses each moment and resides
in every one of us." – Andrew Forsthoefel,
Walking to Listen

DANDELION FLUFF
Kate Louise Brown (1837-1921), published in
The Plant Baby and Its Friends, 1897

O voyager a-sailing
Across the stainless blue,
O happy little traveler!
I long to go with you;
To dance beneath the sunshine
One golden summer hour,
Then seek the brown earth's waiting breast
And someday be a flower.

"Be who you are, and be that perfectly well."
St. Augustine

AUGUST NIGHT

Elizabeth Madox Roberts (1881-1941), published in
Under the Tree, 1922

We had to wait for the heat to pass,

And I was lying on the grass,

While Mother sat outside the door,
And I saw how many stars there were.

Beyond the tree, beyond the air,
And more and more were always there.

So many that I think they must
Be sprinkled on the sky like dust.

A dust is coming through the sky!
And I felt myself begin to cry.

So many of them and so small,
Suppose I cannot know them all.

"If people sat outside and looked at the stars each
night, I'll bet they'd live a lot differently."
Bill Watterson

FIREFLIES
Elizabeth Jenkins (1905-2010),
published in *Best Friends*, 1955

I like the warm dark summer night,

When fireflies burn their golden light,
And flit so softly through the air,
Now up, now down, now over there!

They sparkle in my apple tree,
And from the grass they wink at me,
And turn their lights on one by one;
I think it would be lots of fun
If I could shine at evening, too,
Just as the little fireflies do.

But Mother tells me I can be
A little light for all to see,
A little candle clear and bright
That shines for Jesus day and night.

"We should always endeavor to wonder at the
permanent thing, not at the mere exception. We
should be startled by the sun, and not by the eclipse.
We should wonder less at the earthquake, and
wonder more at the earth." – C. S. Lewis

August 15
The Assumption of the Blessed Virgin Mary

HAIL, O STAR OF THE OCEAN
(Ave Maris Stella)

Attributed variously to Venantius Fortunantus (530-609), and to St. Bernard of Clairvaux (1090-1153), [Hymn for Evening Prayer on this day]

Hail, O Star of the ocean,
God's own Mother blest,
Ever sinless Virgin,
Gate of heaven's rest. . . .
Show thyself a Mother,

May the Word divine,
Born for us thine Infant,
Hear our prayers through thine.

Virgin all excelling,
Mildest of the mild,
Free from guilt preserve us,
Meek and undefiled.

Keep our life all spotless,
Make our way secure
Till we find in Jesus,
Joys that shall endure.

"'Behold, the virgin shall be with child and bear a son, and they shall name him Emmanuel,'" which means 'God is with us.'" – Matthew 1:23

I'M GLAD
Published in *The Humbler Poets*, 1911

I'm glad the sky is painted blue,

And the earth is painted green,
With such a lot of nice fresh air
All sandwiched in between.

WHY THE SKY IS BLUE
Hyacinth Blocker (1904-1969), published in
Locust Bloom and Other Poems, 1938

It must be washday in Heaven Town

To judge by doings in the sky,
For I think I see Our Lady's gown
Hung out upon the clouds to dry!

"Sometimes we see a cloud that's dragonish."
William Shakespeare

FOUR AND EIGHT

Ffrida Wolfe (1893-1974), published in
Everychild: A Book of Verses for Children, 1921

The Foxglove by the cottage door
Looks down on Joe, and Joe is four.
The Foxglove by the garden gate
Looks down on Joan, and Joan is eight.

"I'm glad we're small," said Joan, "I love
To see inside the fox's glove,
Where taller people cannot see,
And all is ready for the bee;
The door is wide, the feast is spread,
The walls are dotted rosy red."
"And only little people know
How nice it looks in there," said Joe.
Said Joan, "The upper rooms are locked;
A bee went buzzing up—he knocked,
But no one let him in, so then
He bumbled gaily down again."
"Oh dear!" sighed Joe, "if only we
Could grow as little as that bee,
We too might room by room explore
The Foxglove by the cottage door."

The Foxglove by the garden gate
Looked down and smiled on Four and Eight.

"We shall not cease from exploration,
And the end of all our exploring
Will be to arrive where we started
And know the place for the first time." – T. S. Eliot

St. Helen

Robert Hugh Benson (1871-1914), published in
An Alphabet of Saints, 1906

"**H**" for ST. HELEN, the Empress who sailed
To find the True Cross, on which JESUS was nailed.
When she set out from Rome she was eighty, but still
In the strength of her faith she reached Calvary Hill;
Where at last, with much digging and delving, she found
Three crosses exactly alike in the ground.
To a woman in pain the three crosses were brought
To see by which cross her relief would be wrought;
In vain were the first and the second applied,
On which the two Robbers had been crucified;
But when the third touched her the woman was healed,
And thus the True Cross of our LORD was revealed.
    This British Princess, who was Empress at Rome,
    Was born, so they say, in a Colchester home;
    As she may have been born there, I think it's a pity
    St. HELEN'S forgotten in Colchester City.

(ST. HELEN or HELENA, Empress, Widow, Mother of the Emperor Constantine; Born in England, per-haps at Colchester, about 245; Died in Rome, 328. Feast, August 18)

"When they came to the place called the Skull, they crucified him and the criminals there, one on his right, the other on his left." – Luke 23:33

BEES

Kate Louise Brown (1837-1921), published in
The Plant Baby and Its Friends, 1897

There's an auction today, just over the way,
And all the bees are coming.
Bum! Bum! Bum! See, now they come!
With all their humming and drumming.

The flags are out, 'tis a merry rout*
And more and more are coming.
"Clover, have you sweets to sell?
Give to me, I'll pay you well,"
The merry bees are humming.

* retreat

"The flower doesn't dream of the bee. It blossoms
and the bee comes." – Mark Nepo

THE SECRET
Abbie Farwell Brown (1871-1927), published in
Songs of Sixpence, 1914

I HEAR God's whisper in the wind,
    And in the roaring sea;
And just as plainly in the grass
    As in the tall pine tree.

He breathes a Secret in my ear;
    Though I am very small,
He says, to Him I am as dear
    As people wise and tall.

"Nature is too thin a screen; the glory of the One
bursts through everywhere." – Ralph Waldo Emerson,
"Nature: A Revelation of God"

THE PINE TREE SWING
Homer H. Harbour (1889-1955), published in
140 Folk Tunes, 1922

Amid the boughs of an old pine tree
I've found me a wonderful swing
Where I can rest so safe, so high,
And hear the breeze in the branches sigh
And up and down, and up and down
The wind sings rock-a-bye.
I lie and watch through the branches;
The white clouds sail lazily by
And sometimes little birds fly near
And sing their songs close to my ear
And up and down, and up and down
I rock between earth and sky.

"You must not blame me if I do talk to the clouds."
Henry David Thoreau

SAINT JOSEPH'S SONG

Rev. Gerald M. C. Fitzgerald (1894-1969), published in
Paths from Bethlehem, 1938

Steadily I work, softly do I sing,
For I serve a queen most fair and a little King:
Angels' lips have told me whence my Treasures
came,
Mary is His mother, Jesus is His name.

Angels oft have whispered how they envy me,
Why the Lord has chosen thus a mystery:
What have I to offer Him save my poverty?

When the sun is setting and my work is done,
Homeward do I hasten, and God's little Son
Comes to rest His golden head 'gainst my tired
one.

Mary lifts her eyes to call me to a poor man's meal—
Blest the bread by her hands kneaded—ever do I
feel
Deeper wonder, deeper reverence o'er my spirit steal.

So my work is sweet, and I softly sing,
For I serve a queen most fair and a little King:
Angels' lips have told me whence my Treasures
came,
Mary is His mother; Jesus is His name.

". . . the angel of the Lord appeared to him in a
dream and said, 'Joseph, son of David, do not be
afraid to take Mary your wife into your home. For it is
through the holy Spirit that this child has been
conceived in her.'" – Matthew 1:20

MOON-SHEEP

Christopher Morley (1890-1957), published in
Chimneysmoke, 1921

The moon seems like a docile sheep,
She pastures while all people sleep;
But sometimes, when she goes astray,
She wanders all alone by day.

Up in the clear blue morning air
We are surprised to see her there,
Grazing in her woolly white,
Waiting the return of night.

When dusk lets down the meadow bars
She greets again her lambs, the stars!

"Not all those who wander are lost." – J. R. Tolkien

POPLARS

James Kinney Collins, published in *Religious
Poems for Little Folks*, 1936

Slim poplars, cutting the night
In the pale moon's dusky light,
Is this gently swaying
Your own way of praying
In the silence of the night,
Like a holy candle's light?
Are you whispering the Name
Like the candle's timid flame?

"By the rivers of Babylon
there we sat weeping
when we remembered Zion.
On the poplars in its midst
we hung up our harps."
Psalms 137:1-2

St. Louis

Robert Hugh Benson (1871-1914), published in
An Alphabet of Saints, 1906

"**L**" for ST. LOUIS, a King without blame,
Who ruled over France as the Ninth of his name.
When LOUIS was given the Crown made of Thorn
Which CHRIST on the Cross of His Passion had worn,
He carried that Most Holy Crown in his hand
From Sens into Paris, barefoot through the land;
Then he got a small piece of the True Cross as well,
And built for these relics *La Sainte Chapelle*.
Now LOUIS fell ill, and they thought he was dead,
But he suddenly rose with new strength from his bed,
And resolving to fight the good fight for our LORD,
Put on his chain-armor, took helmet and sword,
And asked the Archbishop of Paris to bless
The Cross of Crusade that he sewed on his dress.
   In the Crown of a King and the Habit and Cord
   Of St. FRANCIS he died, and was crowned by
      the LORD.

(ST. LOUIS, King of France, Confessor, Penitent of the
Third Order of Saint Francis. Born at Poissy, in France,
1215; Died in Northern Africa, 1270. Feast, August 25.)

"And the soldiers wove a crown out of thorns and
placed it on his head, and clothed him in a purple
cloak," – John 19:2

GLAD DAY

W. Graham Robertson (1867-1948), published in
The Home Book of Verse, 1918

Here's another day, dear,
  Here's the sun again
Peeping in his pleasant way
  Through the window pane.
  Rise and let him in, dear,
  Hail him "Hip hurray!"
Now the fun will all begin.
  Here's another day!

  Down the coppice* path, dear,
  Through the dewy glade,
(When the Morning took her bath
  What a splash she made!)
  Up the wet wood-way, dear,
  Under dripping green
Run to meet another day,
  Brightest ever seen. . . .

  Such a lot to do, dear,
  Such a lot to see!
How we ever can get through
  Fairly puzzles me.
  Hurry up and out, dear,
  Then —away! away!
In and out and round about,
  Here's another day!

* a woodland area that has been cut back

"Ever since the creation of the world, his invisible
attributes of eternal power and divinity have been
able to be understood and perceived in what he has
made. . . ." – Romans 1:20

WHEN A MOUNTING SKYLARK SINGS

Christina Rossetti (1830-1894), published in
Sing Song, A Nursery Rhyme Book, 1872

When a mounting skylark sings
In the sunlit summer morn,
I know that heaven is up on high,
And on the earth are fields of corn.

But when a nightingale sings
In the moonlit summer even,
I know not if earth is merely earth,
Only that heaven is heaven.

"Heaven is under our feet as well as over our heads."
Henry David Thoreau

August 28
St. Augustine

HEART MADE FOR THEE

St. Augustine (354-430), published in
Religious Poems for Little Folks, 1936

Our hearts were made for Thee, O Lord,
And restless must they be
Until—O, Lord, this grace accord!—
Until they rest in Thee.

". . . St. Monica, with her son, when at the port of
Ostia, they were lost in ecstasy at the sight of the
Creator's marvels!" – St. Therese of Lisieux,
Story of a Soul

GOLDENROD
Mrs. F. J. Lovejoy, published in
Nature in Verse, 1896

T ell me, sunny goldenrod,
Growing everywhere,
Did fairies come from fairyland
And make the dress you wear?

Did you get from mines of gold
Your bright and shining hue?
Or did the baby stars some night
Fall down and cover you?

Or did the angels wave their wings
And drop their glitter down
Upon you, laughing goldenrod,
Your nodding head to crown?

Or are you clad in sunshine
Caught from summer's brightest day,
To give again in happy smiles
To all who pass your way?

I love you, laughing goldenrod,
And I will try, like you,
To fill each day with deeds of cheer;
Be loving, kind, and true.

"Some old-fashioned things like fresh air and sunshine
are hard to beat." – Laura Ingalls Wilder

SUNSET

Mary Mabel Wirries (1893-1967), published in *Gay Witch April and Other Poems*, 1936

The mischief Sun ran down the sky
And got into the Rainbow's dye.
He smeared the orange and red and blue.
He dipped into the purple, too.

I stood down in the maple shade
And watched the picture that he made.
But when he saw me there, so still,
He winked, and ducked behind the hill.

Then as I went indoors for tea
Over my shoulder I could see
The Night go tiptoe 'round about
And try to rub the colors out.

"Every sunset brings the promise of a new dawn."
Ralph Waldo Emerson

THE END OF SUMMER

Edna St. Vincent Millay (1892-1950), published in
The Melody of Earth, 1918

When poppies in the garden bleed,
And coreopsis goes to seed,
And pansies, blossoming past their prime,
Grow small and smaller all the time,
When on the mown field, shrunk and dry,
Brown dock and purple thistle lie,
And smoke from forest fires at noon
Can make the sun appear the moon,
When apple seeds, all white before,
Begin to darken in the core,
I know that summer, scarcely here,
Is gone until another year.

"Without the name, any flower is still more or less a
stranger to you." – John Burroughs

Holy Days and Holidays

THE ASCENSION

Sister Mary Josita Belger (1899-1978), published in
Sing a Song of Holy Things, 1945

Forty sunny days had passed
Since Jesus rose again.
The woods were full of singing birds,
And flowers were blooming then.
> And everything was still and sweet,
> The grass was soft and green.
> The Master stood upon the mount.
> His friends could all be seen.

Those loving friends stood all around
Wondering, for He said,
A little while and He would go
To heaven now instead.
> A little while to see Him,
> A little while at most;
> He was going to the Father,
> And would send the Holy Ghost.

They loved to hear Him call them "Friends."
They listened to His word.
And now their hearts were heavy,
At this sad thing they heard.
> But Jesus knew their broken hearts.
> "I will prepare a place,
> That where I go you, too, may come,
> And see Me face to face."

Then Jesus rose into the air,
Passing through a cloud.
They saw no more their Master;
In wonder, low they bowed. . . .

THE COMING OF THE HOLY SPIRIT
Sister Mary Josita Belger (1899-1978), published in
Sing a Song of Holy Things, 1945

When Jesus stood upon the mount
With all His friends nearby,
He promised them that He would send
The Spirit from on high.

And so they prayed from day to day,
Until the time came near.
Mother Mary stayed with them
To keep away all fear.

Suddenly a mighty wind
Blew through the holy place
Where the apostles knelt to pray.
It filled each tiny space.

They saw a tongue of fire rest
Right over every head.
And no one talked just like himself,
But other ways instead.

The Holy Ghost had filled each heart,
Made each a soldier brave.
They went forth now to preach and teach,
And many souls to save.

DEAR MOTHER MARY
Adelaide Proctor (1825-1864)

Dear Mother Mary
As we kneel,
To thy goodness
We appeal.

Guard us, dear Mother,
Through the day,
In all our work
And all our play.

When darkness comes
The day to hide,
May we still feel you
Close beside.

Mother Mary, keep my soul
Pure from every sin,
So my little soul will smile
When He enters in.

THE BLESSED TRINITY

Sister Mary Josita Belger (1899-1978), published in
Sing a Song of Holy Things, 1945

God is one in Persons three—
Father, Son, and Spirit.
I do not know how it can be,
Even though I hear it.

But I believe it just the same,
And call the Persons three
By that all holy Name of names,
The Blessed Trinity.

God the Father gave His Son
To save the world from sin,
And God the Holy Ghost is Love,
And seeks our souls to win.

So when I make the holy cross
Before my prayers, you see,
I show that I believe that God
Is one in Persons three.

THE RANN OF THE THREE
Traditional Irish Prayer

Three folds in my garment,
Yet only one garment I bear.
Three joints in a finger,
Yet only one finger is there.
Three leaves in a shamrock,
Yet only one shamrock I wear.
Frost, ice, and snow,
These three are nothing but water.
Three Persons in God,
Yet only one God is there.

ANIMA CHRISTI
(SOUL OF CHRIST)

Traditional 14th-Century prayer, translated by
Cardinal John Henry Newman (1801-1890)

Soul of Christ, be my sanctification;

Body of Christ, be my salvation;
Blood of Christ, fill all my veins;
Water of Christ's side, wash out my stains;
Passion of Christ, my comfort be;
O good Jesus, listen to me;
In Thy wounds I fain* would hide;
Ne'er to be parted from Thy side;
Guard me, should the foe assail me;
Call me when my life shall fail me;
Bid me come to Thee above,
With Thy saints to sing Thy love,
World without end.
Amen.

* gladly; with pleasure

THE SACRED HEART OF JESUS

Sister Mary Josita Belger (1899-1978), published in
Sing a Song of Holy Things, 1945

At night when all were sleeping
Within the convent walls,
Sister Margaret Mary rose,
And tiptoed through the halls.

Until she reached the chapel room
With dim red light aflame.
There she knelt in holy peace,
And whispered Jesus' Name.

One night when she was kneeling there,
She gave a little start,
For on the altar Jesus stood,
Showing His Sacred Heart.

He told her that He wished
His Sacred Heart were better known,
That He'd bless the homes where pictures
Of that loving Heart were shown.

He complained about the sinful world,
The cold, hard hearts of men,
And He promised help to sinners
Who would turn to Him again.

Through all the days of all her years,
Through every smallest part,
She tried to win this sinful world
For Jesus' Sacred Heart.

Feast of the Immaculate Heart of Mary
Saturday after *Corpus Christi*

TO THE IMMACULATE HEART OF MARY
Janet P. McKenzie

Apart from the heart of Jesus
What heart has felt such pain
As the heart of Mother Mary,
Heart free of sin and stain.

Heart so pure, heart so bright,
Heart unlike all other;
Heart so clean, heart so white,
Heart of our Blessed Mother.

Heart of Immaculate Mary,
Heart pierced by grief and sword,
Convert my heart; incline my heart
To the Heart of our Lord.

Heart made pure, heart made bright,
Heart made like the Other;
Heart made clean, heart made white,
Heart like our Blessed Mother.

Heart that venerates—
My heart a still sanctuary.
Heart that consecrates—
My heart to Jesus through Mary.

THE PATRONAGE OF ST. JOSEPH
Rev. Frederick Faber (1814-1863), published in *The St. Gregory Hymnal and Catholic Choir Book*, 1920

O blessed Saint Joseph, how great was your worth,
The one chosen shadow of God upon earth,
The father of Jesus! Ah then, will you be,
Sweet spouse of our Lady, a father to me?
For you to the pilgrim are father and guide,
And Jesus and Mary felt safe by your side;
Ah, blessed Saint Joseph, how safe I should be,
Sweet spouse of our Lady, if you were with me!

When the treasures of God where unsheltered on
    earth,
Safe keeping was found for them both in your worth;
O father of Jesus, be father to me,
Sweet spouse of our Lady, and I will love thee.

CHUMS
Published in *A Jolly Jingle-Book*, 1913

We're chums, and we love it—dear father and I!
He's tall and grown-up, of course—ever so high!
But *you* don't mind that, though you're little as me;
He always stoops down, or you sit on his knee
When you're chums.

We go for long walks—he says, "Now for a hike!"—
With beautiful talks about things that I like;
Some folks do not care about beetles and toads
And little green snakes that you find in the roads,
But we're chums.

Sometimes mother gets into trouble with me;
She tells him about it, and he says, "I see!"
His arm gets around me, and pretty soon, then,
I'm telling him I'll never do it again,
'Cause we're chums.

We tell all our secrets, and when things go bad
And worry-lines come in his face, I look glad
And get him a-laughing, and smooth them away.
He says, "Little Partner, it's your turn today!"
So we're chums.

SECRETS
Published in *A Jolly Jingle-Book*, 1913

I know a man that's big and tall,
    With glasses on his nose,
And canes and shiny hats and all
    Such grown-up things as those;
But we have secrets I won't tell!
    Here in the nursery,
Before they ring the dinner-bells
    He's just a boy like me.

He comes home from the office, where
    They think he's just a man
The same as they are, with his hair
    All slick and spick and span.
Oh, don't I make it in a mess!
    It makes us scream for joy.
"Sh—sh!" he says, "they mustn't guess
    I'm nothing but a boy!"

And sometimes when the doorbell rings,
    The girl knocks at the door.
"An' is the doctor in?" she sings,
    A dozen times or more.
"Good-by, old man!" he says. "That bell
    Means business. Here's your toy!"
And off he goes. I'll never tell
    He's nothing but a boy.

FIRST FRIDAY AND FIRST SATURDAY MEDITATIONS

WALKING ON THE WATER

Fr. Vincent McNabb (1868-1948), published in
Gospel Rhymes, 1947

I can't see how St. Peter
Had the heart to leave his boat
As if he wasn't any weight
And like a cork could float.

But once the waves bore up his feet
I can't see why he feared:
As if it wasn't JESUS
But a Phantom that appeared.

Perhaps his feet began to fail
When he gave up his hope,
To show us that it's only God
Can make and keep the POPE.

Lord Jesus! Like St. Peter I
Have death's dark waves to pass.
Say "Don't be frightened. Come to ME,"
And o'er death's waves I'll run to THEE
As o'er the green fields of grass.

THE MARRIAGE FEAST

T. V. Nicholas, published in *Gospel Rhymes*, 1947

At the marriage feast of Cana the married pair
    bewailed,
They hadn't ordered wine enough and suddenly it failed;
They'd made a dreadful muddle, yet who so wise as they,
Who'd ask the Guests that matter most on every marriage
    day?

Our Lady told her Son their plight, then bade the waiters
    round
Do whatsoever He might say, and instantly they found
The water from the water pots had changed to sparkling
wine;
So the married pair were happy and the marriage guests
    could dine.

*Dear Lord, forever afterwards that bride and bridegroom
    knew
That whatsoever you might say they both must always do.
When I'm grown up and marry will You come and be my
    Guest
And Mother Mary with You? And my marriage will be
    blest.*

EASTER MORNING

Fr. Vincent McNabb (1868-1943), published in
Gospel Rhymes, 1947

Said three women to each other:
"Who shall roll away the stone,
For even if we were three men
We'd helpless be alone."

Said the Magdalen: "My soul was once
A tomb walled up with sin
But He who made and loved it
Said one word: and entered in.

Her words were hardly ended
When a thunder-clap was heard,
To an Open Tomb three women flew
With hearts and hopes and longings new
As nest-ward flies a bird.

Dear Lord! My sins are not a STONE
With which I dare to cope.
But You can even MOUNTAINS MOVE
As countless Saints, once Sinners, prove:
And so I'm taking hope.

THE SAVIOR
Henry W. Longfellow (1807-1882)

And Him evermore I behold
Walking in Galilee,
Through the cornfields' waving gold
In hamlet, in wood, in wold*,
By the shores of the beautiful sea.
He touches the sightless eyes;
Before Him the demons flee;
To the dead, He says, "Arise,"
To the living, "Follow Me."
And that voice still sounds on
From the centuries that are gone,
To the centuries that shall be!

* moor: wild, open land

MARTHA AND MARY
Annie Johnson Flint (1866-1932)

Martha was busy and hurried,
Serving the Friend divine,
Cleansing the cups and the platters,
Bringing the bread and the wine . . .
For Martha was "cumbered" with serving,
Martha was "troubled" with "things"—
Those that would pass with the using—
She was forgetting her wings.

But Mary was quiet and peaceful,
Learning to love and to live.
Mary was hearing His precepts,
Mary was letting Him give—
Give of the riches eternal,
Treasures of mind and of heart;
Learning the mind of the Master,
Choosing the better part. . . .

Do we strive for "things" in possession,
And toil for the perishing meat,
Neglecting the one thing needful—
Sitting at Jesus' feet?

Service is good when He asks it,
Labor is right in its place,
But there is one thing better—
Looking up into His face;
There is so much He would tell us,
Truths that are precious and deep;
This is the place where He wants us,
These are the things we can keep.

AFTER HOLY COMMUNION
Sister Mary Josita Belger (1899-1978), published in
Sing a Song of Holy Things, 1945

You have come, my little King,
You're in my heart right now.
To thank You for this visit
I do not know just how.
I welcome you into my heart
I love Your blessed smile.
I know You left all heaven's joys
To be with me a while.

I've tried each day to make my soul
All beautiful and bright.
I've done the things I knew would be
Most pleasing in Your sight.
Thank You! Thank You, Jesus dear.
I give my heart to You.
Bless me and all the friends I love,
And make them happy, too.

ADDITIONAL RESOURCES

WHEN MOTHER READS ALOUD

Hannah G. Fernald (1875-1967), published in
"St. Nicholas" magazine, November 1905

When Mother reads aloud the past
    Seems real as every day;
I hear the tramp of armies vast,
I see the spears and lances cast,
    I join the thrilling fray;
Brave knights and ladies fair and proud
I meet when Mother reads aloud.

When Mother reads aloud, far lands
    Seem very near and true;
I cross the desert's gleaming sands,
Or hunt the jungle's prowling bands,
    Or sail the ocean blue;
Far heights, whose peaks the cold mists shroud,
I scale, when Mother reads aloud.

When Mother reads aloud I long
    For noble deeds to do—
To help the right, redress the wrong,
It seems so easy to be strong,
    So simple to be true,
O, thick and fast the visions crowd
When Mother reads aloud.

RECOMMENDED SUMMER PICTURE BOOKS

STELLAR BOOKS

★Aliki. *Quiet in the Garden* – A little boy observes and hears much as he sits quietly in the garden.

★Baylor, Byrd. *The Other Way to Listen* – Learning to listen to and connect with nature is an important skill to learn.

★Brandenburg, Claire. *The Monk Who Grew Prayer* – This short, colorful book teaches us about the Divine Office—the Liturgy of the Hours—and how we can daily grow prayer everywhere.

★Cooney, Barbara. *Miss Rumphius* – In this beautiful book—with illustrations to match—we learn an important message about the heart of an artist and about life itself. What will you do to make the world a more beautiful place?

INSPECTING GOD'S GLORIOUS CREATION (NATURALIST)

Arnowsky, Jim. *Beachcombing: Exploring the Seashore* – Filled with facts and pictures, this book will allow young beachcombers to identify their seashore treasures.

Barker, Cicely Mary. *A Treasury of Flower Fairies* – With informative poems and evocative watercolor illustrations, this collection teaches us many interesting facts about trees and flowers.

Bateman, Donna R. *Deep in the Swamp* – With bold illustrations, this book provides a description of the gifts of selected swamp animals.

Bogue, Gary. *There's a Hummingbird in My Backyard* – Once the Baker family discovers that hummingbirds live in their backyard, they set out to learn more about them and how to provide for their needs. Look carefully. Are hummingbirds living in *your* backyard?

Cole, Henry. *I Took a Walk* – Learn to identify God's creation in the woods, meadow, stream, and pond with this simply written, nature-search book.

dePaola, Tomie. *The Cloud Book* – Learn about ten different types of clouds and how to predict the weather in this gentle book.

Fleischman, Paul. *Joyful Noise: Poems for Two Voices* – Winner of the esteemed Newbery Medal, this book of poetry in two parts praises the earth's insects.

Fredericks, Anthony D. *Near One Cattail: Turtles, Logs, and Leaping Frogs* – With rhymes that increase in length and rich illustrations, this book presents the variety of creatures in a wetlands environment. Read and learn— then explore for yourself!

George, William. *Box Turtle at Long Pond* – A day in the life of a box turtle is presented with interesting text and vibrant photographs.

Hurst, Carol. *Rocks in His Head* – A man's obsession with collecting rocks teaches him much and, crazy as it seems to others, pays off in the end.

Keats, Ezra. *Over in the Meadow* – With vivid illustrations, this book specifies the gifts of various meadow animals and insects. What do you do to give glory to God?

Kochanoff, Peggy. *You Can Be a Nature* Detective – Tracking, moths and butterflies, frogs and toads, spiders, birds, insects—all of these are included plus a few activities. This is a fun beginning book.

Locker, Thomas. *Cloud Dance* – Beautiful water-colored illustrations with an appendix that teaches about the various types of clouds

Mitchell, Andrew. *The Young Naturalist: An Usborne Guide* – For older readers, this brief book is a great introduction to natural history. In addition to general information, it also contains some experiments.

Sidman, Joyce. *Butterfly Eyes and Other Secrets of the Meadow* – Through riddles and stunning illustrations, discover the hidden world of the meadow.

Wildsmith, Brian. *Owl and the Woodpecker* – Two birds learn to co-exist despite their different sleeping habits.

Worth, Valerie. *Animal Poems* – Twenty-three free-verse poems with rich cut-paper illustrations explore the unique attributes of each animal.

Wood, Douglas. *No One But You* – No one but Douglas Wood can so uniquely challenge us to experience nature as only each one of us as individuals can.

Yolen, Jane. *Bug Off: Creepy, Crawly Poems* – With stunning photographs, these thirteen poems are full of fun and factual information.

RESPECTING GOD'S CREATION
(ECO-CATHOLIC)

Dunlap, Julie. *Louisa May & Mr. Thoreau's Flute* – In Mr. Henry David Thoreau, Louisa May Alcott discovers a companion in her love for the great outdoors and finally finds a voice for her writing.

Emerson, Ralph. *Father, We Thank You* – Gratitude is expressed for many aspects of nature through a hike and campout in the hills and woods.

Locker, Thomas. *John Muir, America's Naturalist* – This simple biography has stunning landscapes and numerous quotations of John Muir.

Slade, Suzanne. *Out of School and into Nature: The Story of Anna Comstock* – Illustrated with beautiful watercolors, this is a short biography of an artist and naturalist who defied the concept of her day that women do not study and teach science and natural history.

REFLECTING ON THE MYSTERY OF GOD
(MYSTIC)

Blake, Robert J. *The Perfect Spot* – A boy and his father search for the perfect spot in the woods. Where is your perfect spot?

Browne, Michael. *Give Her the River: A Father's Wish for His Daughter* – In this lyrical reflection on love and nature, the greatest gift a father can give to his beloved daughter is the changing moods and seasons of the river.

dePaola, Tomie. *Quiet* – A simple book that teaches a simple message: "To be quiet and still is a special thing."

Frost, Helen. *Step Gently Out* – Stunning photographs accompany a gentle nature poem that points out all the small creatures in our world.

MacLachlan, Patricia. *All the Places to Love* – This reverential book expresses a farm family's deep connection to nature, to life, and to family—beautifully done.

Paulsen, *Canoe Days* – A gentle, peaceful book that accurately captures the experience of canoeing with descriptive text and vivid pictures

DETECTING GOD IN NATURE
(NATURE DETECTIVE)

Bunting, Eve. *Anna's Table* – Anna collects beauties from nature and saves them for her "nature table" in her bedroom.

Gibbons, Gail. *Sun Up, Sun Down* – Simple text and pictures explain the fun and function of the sun.

Goudey, Alice. E. *The Day We Saw the Sun Come Up* – In this informative Caldecott Honor book, two children get up before sunrise and learn about the sun and how it works.

Hanna, Julie. *The Man Who Named the Clouds* – An interesting biography of Luke Howard (1772-1864), this weather history book teaches us how the types of clouds were named and encourages us to keep a weather journal.

Lepp, Bil. *The King of Little Things* – This interesting tale teaches us that little things—things that we often deem as too little to be important—have a place, function, and power in the Kingdom of God.

Voake, Steve. *Insect Detective* – Learn how to slip outside and discover the insects around you and the good they are doing for the earth.

GENERAL NATURE BOOKS

Arnosky, Jim. *Crinkleroot's Guide to Walking in Wild Places* – Crinkleroot shares not only the joys of woods walking but possible pitfalls such as poison ivy and oak, ticks, and bees/wasps.

Casanova,Mary. *Wake Up, Island* – Awaken each morning to the wonders of nature with this gentle, magical North Woods island poem.

Florian, Douglas. *Summersaults* – A book of fun and funny summer poems

Hoberman, Mary Ann (editor). *Forget-Me-Nots: Poems to Learn by Heart* – With many poems about nature, this collection for children contains 120 poems from both classical and contemporary poets.

Hopkinson, Deborah. *Bluebird Summer* – In memory of their grandmother, two children cultivate flowers and plant a birdhouse.

James, Simon. *The Birdwatchers* – In this humorous book, we find a young girl accompanying her grandfather on one of his bird-watching walks. The illustrations (and ending) are sure to delight.

LaMarche, Jim. *Raft* – A boy discovers a raft when he visits his grandma for what he thought would be a boring summer.

Locker, Thomas. *Where the River Begins* – Two boys and their grandfather hike to the source of the river that flows by their house.

Macken, JoAnn Early. *Waiting Out the Storm* – A lyrical lullaby, the lush, reassuring illustrations of this book soothe while the text educates and demonstrates what the animals do during a storm. There is nothing to fear.

McCloskey, Robert. *Time of Wonder* – Another Caldecott Medal winner, this book, with vibrant pictures, poetically portrays a young family's life on a Maine island as they prepare to leave at the end of summer.

Owens, Mary Beth. *Be Blest: A Celebration of Seasons* – A delightful celebration of each month of the year with poetry and exquisite illustrations

Polacco, Patricia. *Thunder Cake* – Grandma teaches her grandchild not to be afraid of the sound of thunder by making a special cake; the recipe is included.

Sandved, Kjeli. *Butterfly Alphabet Book* – Accompanied with short poems, these amazing photographs of actual butterfly wings depict each letter of the alphabet.

Schnur, Steven. *Summer: An Alphabet Acrostic* – Using words that emphasize warm-weather delights, this book is an interesting approach to a summer book.

Stevenson, Robert L. and Gyo Fujikawa. *A Child's Garden of Verses* – These familiar poems are graced with the sweet and simple illustrations of Gyo Fujikawa.

Tudor, Tasha. *Around the Year* – A walk through a country year with Tasha Tudor's usual, delightful illustrations.

Udry, Janice May. *The Moon Jumpers* – Starry skies and a moonlit night, along with Maurice Sendak's enchanting artwork, fill this Caldecott Honor book with the wonder of nature.

Udry, Janice May. *A Tree Is Nice* – This Caldecott Award winner describes all the various benefits of a tree—simple and cute.

Wallner, Alexandra. *Lucy Maud Montgomery, The Author of Anne of Green Gables* – With plentiful illustrations, this short biography tells how a determined and imaginative young girl often turned to nature and her stories in her loneliness. How can our personal experiences and background enrich our gifts and what we have to offer to others?

Whelan, Gloria. *Jam & Jelly by Holly & Nellie* – Can Holly get a warm coat so she can go to school?

Zolstow, Charlotte. *When the Wind Stops* – When a little boy is sad that the day will end, his mother shares with him the comfort of the continuity of each day, each season, indeed, all of life.

FAVORITE CHILDREN'S NATURE POETS

Below is a very short list of great poets who composed many wonderful nature poems. Search for their various poetry books online or read their poems from a poetry website.

de la Mare, Walter
Farjeon, Eleanor
Fisher, Aileen
Florian, Douglas
Rossetti, Christina
Sidman, Joyce

Silverstein, Shel
Singer, Marilyn
Stevenson, Robert Louis
Wynne, Annette
Yolen, Jane

COLLECTABLE CHILDREN'S POETRY BOOKS

These books are out of print but are worth collecting, especially the Catholic books.

Child on His Knees, The (Mary Dixon Thayer, 1948)

Lovely Gate Set Wide (A): A Book of Catholic Verse for Young People (Sr. Margaret Patrice, 1946)

Nature in Verse (Compiled by Mary Lovejoy, 1895)

Religious Poems for Little Folks (Bruce Publishing Company, 1936)

Sing a Song of Holy Things (Sr. Mary Josita, 1945)

Songs of the Tree-Top and Meadow (Collected and Arranged by Lida Brown McMurry and Agnes Spofford Cook, 1899)

With Harp and Lute (Blanche Jennings Thompson, 1935)

A FEW CHILDREN'S POETRY ANTHOLOGIES

All the Silver Pennies (Edited by Blanche Jennings Thompson)

Book of 1,000 Poems, The

Favorite Poems: Old and New (Selected by Helen Ferris)

National Geographic Book of Nature Poetry: More than 200 Poems With Photographs That Float, Zoom, and Bloom! (Edited by J. Patrick Lewis)

Poems for Memorization (Rod and Staff Publishers)

Read-Aloud Poems for the Very Young (Selected by Jack Prelutsky)

Sing a Song of Seasons: A Nature Poem for Each Day of the Year (Selected by Fiona Waters)

The Random House Book of Poetry for Children: A Treasure of 572 Poems for Today's Child (Selected by Jack Prelutsky)

RECOMMENDED ADULT RESOURCES

The following lists of books are intended to aid you in becoming more confident as a nature mentor and student of natural history. This subject used to be taught in schools along with reading, writing, and 'rithmetic. In addition, years ago people were more connected to nature through farming, gardening, and general rural living. Scott Sampson states, "By the close of the 1900s, most Americans could describe themselves as naturalists" (*How to Raise a Wild Child*). Browse through the lists and pick at least one book from each category to educate and inspire you. Most books can be found in your local library or purchased new or used online.

The "Why" of Nature

- 📖 *Last Child in the Woods: Saving Our Children from Nature-Deficit Disorder* by Richard Louv
- 📖 *Step into Nature: Nurturing Imagination and Spirit in Everyday Life* by Patrice Vecchione
- 📖 *The Joyful Mystery: Field Notes toward a Green Thomism* by Christopher J. Thompson
- 📖 *The Nature Fix: Why Nature Makes Us Happier, Healthier, and More Creative* by Florence Williams

Connection with Nature

- 📖 *A Blessing of Toads: A Guide to Living with Nature* by Sharon Lovejoy
- 📖 *How to Be a Wildflower: A Field Guide* by Katie Daisy
- 📖 *The Curious Nature Guide: Explore the Natural Wonders All Around You* by Clare Walker Leslie
- 📖 *The Secret Wisdom of Nature: Trees, Animals, and the Extraordinary Balance of All Living Things* by Peter Wohlleben

📖 *What the Robin Knows: How Birds Reveal the Secrets of the Natural World* by Jon Young

Nature Activity Books—Outdoor Adventuring

📖 *15 Minutes Outside: 365 Ways to Get Out of the House and Connect with Your Kids* by Rebecca P. Cohen [elementary age]

📖 *Go Wild! 101 Things to Do Outdoors before You Grow Up* by Jo Schofield and Fiona Danks [teens]

📖 *Hands-On Nature: Information and Activities for Exploring the Environment with Children* by Jenepher Lingelbach [Grades K-6]

📖 *I Love Dirt: 52 Activities to Help You and Your Kids Discover the Wonders of Nature* by Jennifer Ward [ages 4-8]

📖 *Roots, Shoots, Buckets & Boots: Gardening Together with Children* by Sharon Lovejoy

📖 *Teaching Kids to Love the Earth: Sharing a Sense of Wonder . . . 186 Outdoor Activities for Parents and Other Teachers* by Herman, Passineau, Schimpf, & Treuer [all ages]

📖 *The Boy's Book of Adventure: The Little Guidebook for Smart and Resourceful Boys* by Michele Lecreux [for girls too!]

📖 *The Wild Weather Book: Loads of Things to Do Outdoors in Rain, Wind and Snow* by Fiona Danks and Jo Schofield

📖 *Vitamin N: The Essential Guide to a Nature-Rich Life—500 Ways to Enrich the Health & Happiness of Your Family & Community* by Richard Louv

Nature Journaling

📖 *Drawn to Nature through the Journals of Clare Walker Leslie*

   📖 *Keeping a Nature Journal: Discover a Whole New Way of Seeing the World Around You* by Clare Walker Leslie & Charles E. Roth [ideas and "how to"]

   📖 *Nature Journal: A Guided Journal for Illustrating and Recording Your Observations of the Natural World* with Clare Walker Leslie

   📖 *The Country Diary of an Edwardian Lady* by Edith Holden

   📖 *The Naturalist's Notebook for Tracking Changes in the Natural World Around You* by Nathaniel T. Wheelwright & Bernd Heinrich

Nature Crafts and Drawing Books

   📖 *Crafting with Nature: Grow or Gather Your Own Supplies for Simple Handmade Crafts, Gifts & Recipes* by Amy Renea

   📖 *Make It Wild: 101 Things to Make and Do Outdoors* by Fiona Danks and Jo Schofield

   📖 *Nature Crafts for Kids: 50 Fantastic Things to Make with Mother Nature's Help* by Gwen Diehn & Terry Krautwurst

   📖 *Peggy Dean's Guide to Nature Drawing and Watercolor: Learn to Sketch, Ink, and Paint Flowers, Plants, Trees, and Animals* by Peggy Dean

Nature Books for Grandparents

   📖 *Granny Camp by Sharon Lovejoy*

   📖 *The Rhythm of Family: Discovering a Sense of Wonder through the Seasons* by Amanda Blake Soule with Stephen Soule

   📖 *Toad Cottages & Shooting Stars: Grandma's Bag of Tricks* by Sharon Lovejoy

The Practice of *Shinrin-yoku:* Forest Therapy or Forest Bathing
- 📖 *Your Guide to Forest Bathing: Experience the Healing Power of Nature* by M. Amos Clifford
- 📖 Review the teaching philosophies of educators such as Maria Montessori and Charlotte Mason

The Practice of Mindfulness
- 📖 *A Catholic Guide to Mindfulness* by Susan Brinkmann, OCDS
- 📖 *The Mindful Catholic: Finding God One Moment at a Time* by Dr Gregory Bottaro
- 📖 *The Practice of the Presence of God* by Br. Lawrence of the Resurrection
- 📖 *The Sacrament of the Present Moment* by Jean-Pierre de Caussade (also published as *Abandonment to Divine Providence*)

"For if they so far succeeded in knowledge that they could speculate about the world, how did they not more quickly find its Lord?"

Wisdom 13:9

Appendix

Seeking God in Nature with the Church

ASSURANCES AND GENERAL COUNSELS: SEEKING GOD IN NATURE VS. NATURE WORSHIP

With the advent of the New Age Movement or New Age Spirituality, many Catholics have become rightfully cautious regarding seeking God (and praying with Him) in nature as this book series promotes. In order to reassure you and provide some general counsel and advice, the following "lessons" are provided regarding the proper place the reverence of God has in His creation and the appropriateness of communing with Him in the natural world. Below are various appropriate passages from the *Catechism of the Catholic Church*, papal documents, and teachings of the United States bishops. By following the guidelines established with these various Church authorities, we can be assured not to go astray or to lead others down a questionable path of holiness.

Remember these basic principles when using the natural world to converse with God and advance in the life of prayer:

1. God is distinct from His creation. A tree is not God, but can help us better understand the attributes, love, and mercy of God.
2. While it is our intent to learn more about the natural world, this knowledge is for the sole purpose of uniting ourselves closer to the living God, the God of all creation.
3. There is nothing that exists that was not created by God—with a purpose. By understanding the uniqueness of each individual creation, its God-given purpose, and its connection to the rest of

creation, we can learn much about God and our relationship with Him and His creation.

4. God wants you to be surrounded with truth, beauty, and goodness. Creation gives us a glimpse of these features of God and fills us with gratitude.

5. The sole purpose of our existence is to unite our will perfectly with the Will of God and so attain perfect happiness in heaven. Any thing, any person, or any "method" or means of prayer that impedes our goal of uniting ourselves with the Triune God by increasing our self-centeredness or deflecting the reverence that belongs to God to any other person or object is not in accordance with divine teaching or the authority of the Catholic Church.

I promote communing with God in the natural world as it has worked unfailingly for me throughout my life—even as a professed Secular Carmelite. God speaks in eternal silence and in holy silence must be heard by the soul. This silence is often found in the stillness of the natural world. Matthew Kelly often speaks of spending time in the "classroom of silence." For me, nature provides the best classroom—free of the distractions of daily life.

If I spend too little time in silence with God in nature, my peace quickly evaporates, just as not frequenting the sacraments or spending too little time with Jesus in the Blessed Sacrament of the Altar does.

What drew me as a convert to the Catholic Church is the Church's vast array of available means to attain holiness. Perhaps this method of communing with the God of the universe will assist you—and your loved ones as well—along the path of holiness. That is my deep desire.

A BRIEF LESSON ON NEW AGE SPIRITUALITY

While the gamut of New Age spirituality is vast and is composed of a variety of theologies, consider the following generally accepted principles of this philosophy: (Note that all of these are in conflict with the teachings of the Catholic Church.)

- No central authority or teaching, no formal doctrine, or membership
- Contains part of many "isms" such as Pantheism (All things are divine.), Gnosticism (salvation by knowledge), and occultism (knowledge or use of supernatural forces or beings)
- God and creation are one. There is no separation between them.
- Christ is a type of energy, not necessarily an individual being.
- Morality is individually determined—moral relativism
- Influenced by Eastern religions and forms of meditation
- Man is divine and perfected through reincarnation.

For our purposes, remember that God and creation are not one. Creation is a *reflection* of God and can help us come to know Him better. Knowledge of the natural world serves to draw us into closer union with the Creator as we come to see the diversity, beauty, and goodness of nature. We can become more deeply connected to God —and grow in gratitude for His constant presence and many gifts—when we see His hand in the world around us and can pray gratefully to Him in the silence of creation. We can join with all creation to sing praise to the glory of our loving God!

LESSONS FROM THE *CATECHISM OF THE CATHOLIC CHURCH*

The following are excerpts from the *Catechism* regarding God and the natural (visible) world that should assure us that this path of union with God is trustworthy and in full communion with the Holy See:

¶32 . . . As St. Paul says of the Gentiles: For what can be known about God is plain to them, because God has shown it to them. Ever since the creation of the world his invisible nature, namely, his eternal power and deity, has been clearly perceived in the things that have been made (Rom 1:19-20; cf., Acts 14:15, 17; 17:27-28; Wis 13:1-9). And St. Augustine issues this challenge: Question the beauty of the earth, question the beauty of the sea, question the beauty of the air distending and diffusing itself, question the beauty of the sky . . . question all these realities. All respond: "See, we are beautiful." Their beauty is a profession [*confessio*]. These beauties are subject to change. Who made them if not the Beautiful One [Pulcher] who is not subject to change? (St. Augustine, *Sermo* 241, 2: Patrologia Latina 38, 1134)

¶41 All creatures bear a certain resemblance to God, most especially man, created in the image and likeness of God. The manifold perfections of creatures—their truth, their goodness, their beauty all reflect the infinite perfection of God. Consequently we can name God by taking his creatures' perfections as our starting point, "for from the greatness and beauty of created things comes a corresponding perception of their Creator" (Wisdom 13:5).

¶293 Scripture and Tradition never cease to teach and celebrate this fundamental truth: "The world was made for the glory of God" (*Dei Filius*, can. # 5: S 3025). St. Bonaventure explains that God created all things "not to increase his glory, but to show it forth and to communicate it" (St. Bonaventure, *In II Sent.* I, 2, 2, 1), for God has no other reason for creating than his love and goodness: "Creatures came into existence when the key of love opened his hand" (St. Thomas Aquinas, *Sent. II*, prol.). The First Vatican Council explains:

This one, true God, of his own goodness and "almighty power", not for increasing his own beatitude, nor for attaining his perfection, but in order to manifest this perfection through the benefits which he bestows on creatures, with absolute freedom of counsel "and from the beginning of time, made out of nothing both orders of creatures, the spiritual and the corporeal. . ." (13 *Dei Filius* I: DS 3002; cf Lateran Council IV (1215): DS 800.7)

¶294 The glory of God consists in the realization of this manifestation and communication of his goodness, for which the world was created. . . ."

GOD TRANSCENDS CREATION AND IS PRESENT TO IT

¶300 God is infinitely greater than all his works: "You have set your glory above the heavens" (Ps 8:1; cf. Sir 43:28). Indeed, God's "greatness is unsearchable" (Ps 145:3). But because he is the free and sovereign Creator, the first cause of all that exists, God is present to his creatures' inmost being: "In him we live and move and have our being" (Acts 17:28). In the words of St. Augustine, God is "higher than my highest and more inward than my innermost self" (St. Augustine, Conf: 3, 6, 11: PL 32, 688). God upholds and sustains creation.

¶337 God himself created the visible world in all its richness, diversity and order. . . . On the subject of creation, the sacred text teaches the truths revealed by God for our salvation (*Dei Verbum* Cf. 11), permitting us to "recognize the inner nature, the value and the ordering of the whole of creation to the praise of God" (*Lumen Gentium* 36 #2).

¶338 Nothing exists that does not owe its existence to God the Creator. . . .

¶339 Each creature possesses its own particular goodness and perfection. . . . Each of the various creatures, willed in its own being, reflects in its own way a ray of God's infinite wisdom and goodness. Man must therefore respect the particular goodness of every creature, to avoid any disordered use of things which would be in contempt of the Creator and would bring disastrous consequences for human beings and their environment.

¶340 God wills the interdependence of creatures: the sun and the moon, the cedar and the little flower, the eagle and the sparrow: the spectacle of their countless diversities and inequalities tells us that no creature is self-sufficient. Creatures exist only in dependence on each other, to complete each other, in the service of each other.

¶341 The beauty of the universe: the order and harmony of the created world results from the diversity of beings and from the relationships which exist among them. Man discovers them progressively as the laws of nature. They call forth the admiration of scholars. The beauty of creation reflects the infinite beauty of the Creator and ought to inspire the respect and submission of man's intellect and will.

¶344 There is a solidarity among all creatures arising from the fact that all have the same Creator and are all ordered to his glory . . .

¶2416 *Animals* are God's creatures. He surrounds them with his providential care. By their mere existence they bless him and give him glory (Cf. Mt 6:26; Dan 3:79-81). Thus men owe them kindness. We should recall the gentleness with which saints like St. Francis of Assisi or St. Philip Neri treated animals.

LESSONS FROM RECENT PAPAL DOCUMENTS

One of the earliest papal documents to call attention to the environment is Pope Saint Paul VI's 1971 letter, *Octogesima Adveniens,* his reflection on the challenges of the post-industrial society. Here, he calls the environment a "wide-ranging social problem which concerns the entire human family" (¶21). Pope Saint John Paul II again addresses ecological matters in the 1988 *Sollicitudo Socialis (On Social Concern)*; and, in 1990, became the first pope to devote an entire papal document to the environmental issue: "Peace with God the Creator, Peace with All of Creation" (1990)—a document well worth reading. An entire chapter of *The Compendium of the Social Doctrine of the Church* (2004) addresses the topic of "Safeguarding the Environment." This chapter was condensed into "The Ten Commandments for the Environment" by Bishop Giampaolo Crepaldi in 2005.

Pope Benedict XVI spent so much of his papacy promoting an environmental message through addresses, encyclicals, and scientific conferences that he became known as the "Green Pope." Pope Francis has spoken frequently about ecological concerns and addressed his 2015 encyclical *Laudato Si': On Care for Our Common*

Home not just to a Catholic audience but to "every person living on this planet" (¶3).

For our purposes, however, let us limit our study to those papal references that especially address seeking and praising God in creation.

"PEACE WITH GOD THE CREATOR, PEACE WITH ALL OF CREATION" (Pope Saint John Paul II, 1990):

¶13 An education in ecological responsibility is urgent . . . The first educator, however, is the family, where the child learns to respect his neighbor and to love nature.

¶14 Finally, the aesthetic value of creation cannot be overlooked. Our very contact with nature has a deep restorative power; contemplation of its magnificence imparts peace and serenity. The Bible speaks again and again of the goodness and beauty of creation, which is called to glorify God . . .

¶16 It is my hope that the inspiration of Saint Francis will help us to keep ever alive a sense of "fraternity" with all those good and beautiful things which Almighty God has created. And may he remind us of our serious obligation to respect and watch over them with care, in light of that greater and higher fraternity that exists within the human family.

COMPENDIUM OF THE SOCIAL DOCTRINE OF THE CHURCH (2004):

¶487 The attitude that must characterize the way man acts in relation to creation is essentially one of gratitude and appreciation; the world, in fact, reveals the mystery of God who created and sustains it. If the relationship with God is placed aside, nature is stripped of its profound meaning and impoverished. If on the other hand,

nature is rediscovered in its creaturely dimension, channels of communication with it can be established, its rich and symbolic meaning can be understood, allowing us to enter into its realm of *mystery*. This realm opens the path of man to God, Creator of heaven and earth. *The world presents itself before man's eyes as evidence of God*, the place where his creative, providential and redemptive power unfolds.

CARITAS IN VERITATE (Pope Benedict XVI, 2009): ¶48 ". . . Nature speaks to us of the Creator (cf. Romans 1:20) and his love for humanity."

MEETING WITH PRIESTS AND DEACONS—August 6, 2008, Pope Benedict XVI: "If we observe what came into being around monasteries, how in those places small paradises, oases of creation were and continue to be born, it becomes evident that these were not only words. Rather, wherever the Creator's Word was properly understood, wherever life was lived with the redeeming Creator, people strove to save creation and not to destroy it."

LAUDATO SI' (Pope Francis, 2015):

¶85 "From panoramic vistas to the tiniest living form, nature is a constant source of wonder and awe. It is also a continuing revelation of the divine." . . . "To sense each creature singing the hymn of its existence is to live joyfully in God's love and hope." This contemplation of creation allows us to discover in each thing a teaching which God wishes to hand on to us, "for the believer, to contemplate creation is the hear a message, to listen to a paradoxical and silent voice."

¶87 When we can see God reflected in all that exists, our hearts are moved to praise the Lord for all his creatures and to worship him in union with them.

¶97 As he [Jesus] made his way throughout the land, he often stopped to contemplate the beauty sown by his Father, and invited his disciples to perceive a divine message in things . . .

¶233 The universe unfolds in God, who fills it completely. Hence, there is a mystical meaning to be found in a leaf, in a mountain trail, in a dewdrop, in a poor person's face. The ideal is not only to pass from the exterior to the interior to discover the action of God in the soul, but also to discover God in all things.

¶234 ". . . the mystic experiences the intimate connection between God and all beings, and thus feels that all things are God." Standing awestruck before a mountain, he or she cannot separate this experience from God, and perceives that the interior awe being lived has to be entrusted to the Lord . . .

¶246 . . . Teach us to discover the worth of each thing, to be filled with awe and contemplation, to recognize that we are profoundly united with every creature as we journey towards your infinite light.

LESSONS FROM THE UNITED STATES CONFERENCE OF CATHOLIC BISHOPS

In 1991, the United States Conference of Catholic Bishops published *Renewing the Earth: An Invitation to Reflection and Action on Environment in Light of Catholic Social Teaching,* and, in 2001, *Global Climate Change: A Plea for Dialogue, Prudence, and the Common Good.* Let us examine some excerpts from the former document.

For many people, the environmental movement has reawakened appreciation of the truth that, through the created gifts of nature, men and women encounter their

Creator. The Christian vision of a sacramental universe —a world that discloses the Creator's presence by visible and tangible signs—can contribute to making the earth a home for the human family once again. Pope John Paul II has called for Christians to respect and protect the environment, so that through nature people can "contemplate the mystery of the greatness and love of God. . . . Dwelling in the presence of God, we begin to experience ourselves as part of creation, as stewards within it, not separate from it. As faithful stewards, fullness of life comes from living responsibly within God's creation (III-A).

Nature shares in God's goodness, and contemplation of its beauty and richness raised our hearts and minds to God. . . . Through the centuries, Catholic theologians and philosophers, like St. Paul before them, continue to search for God in reasoning about the created world (IV-A).

We remind *parents* that they are the first and principal teachers of children. It is from parents that children will learn love of the earth and delight in nature. It is at home that they develop the habits of self-control, concern, and care that lie at the heart of environmental morality (V-B).

TWO CURRENT PRACTICES

Seeking God and communing with Him in nature raises several potential "red flags" regarding two currently popular practices: the Japanese practice of *shinrin-yoku*, or forest therapy (forest bathing) and mindfulness.

Many scientific studies show that spending time in nature can have a positive effect on us physically, emotionally, and spiritually. Forest therapy, a concept practiced instinctively for eons, has fallen from practice in modern times. Spending refreshing periods of time with God in the natural world can be spiritually empowering. Organized "immersions" are becoming popular. Be cautious and aware, ensuring that the focus centers on God the Creator—source of all existence.

Mindfulness, derived from a Buddhist meditation technique, also has the potential to lead a Catholic astray. Although similar to the accepted Catholic practices of the Practice of the Presence of God and the Sacrament of the Present Moment, Buddhist mindfulness is centered on the mind; Catholic meditation always centers on God. We want to treasure each moment with God in the natural world, but only in a way that leads us directly to Him.

Educate yourself regarding these two practices by reading one or more of the resources suggested in the Appendix, or research these practices online.

As we deepen our connection with nature—and therefore with our loving God—let us try to develop a "sacramental imagination." According to Mary C. Boys, this is a "vision that sees all creation as mediating the divine." This vision may be easier for children than adults. To seek God through His creation, search for His reflection —consider what each creation can teach us about God, and embrace each gift of nature as a continuation of the mystery that is God: "Even when he reveals himself, God remains a mystery beyond words: 'If you understood him, it would not be God'" *(CCC* ¶230 quoting St. Augustine).

Immerse yourself in nature. Ponder in holy silence His wondrous creation. In all things, give Him glory. Give thanks.

www.ingramcontent.com/pod-product-compliance
Lightning Source LLC
Chambersburg PA
CBHW031257090426
42742CB00007B/501